The Metamorphoses of Ovid

Text by
Dalma Hunyadi Brunauer
(Ph.D., University of Budapest)
Department of Liberal Studies
Clarkson University
Potsdam, New York

Illustrations by
Jerilyn Harney-Baker

Research & Education Association

MAXnotes® for
THE METAMORPHOSES OF OVID

Printed in the United States of America

Library of Congress Catalog Card Number 96-67410

International Standard Book Number 0-87891-027-1

MAXnotes® is a registered trademark of
Research & Education Association, Piscataway, New Jersey 08854

What **MAXnotes**® *Will Do for You*

This book is intended to help you absorb the essential contents and features *The Metamorphoses of Ovid* and to help you gain a thorough understanding of the work. The book has been designed to do this more quickly and effectively than any other study guide.

For best results, this **MAXnotes** book should be used as a companion to the actual work, not instead of it. The interaction between the two will greatly benefit you.

To help you in your studies, this book presents the most up-to-date interpretations of every section of the actual work, followed by questions and fully explained answers that will enable you to analyze the material critically. The questions also will help you to test your understanding of the work and will prepare you for discussions and exams.

Meaningful illustrations are included to further enhance your understanding and enjoyment of the literary work. The illustrations are designed to place you into the mood and spirit of the work's settings.

The **MAXnotes** also include summaries, character lists, explanations of plot, and section-by-section analyses. A biography of the author and discussion of the work's historical context will help you put this literary piece into the proper perspective of what is taking place.

The use of this study guide will save you the hours of preparation time that would ordinarily be required to arrive at a complete grasp of this work of literature. You will be well prepared for classroom discussions, homework, and exams. The guidelines that are included for writing papers and reports on various topics will prepare you for any added work which may be assigned.

The **MAXnotes** will take your grades "to the max."

Dr. Max Fogiel
Program Director

Contents

**Each Book includes List of Characters,
Summary, Analysis, Study Questions and
Answers, and Suggested Essay Topics.**

SECTION ONE

Introduction

The Life and Work of Ovid

The title, *Metamorphoses*, is Greek and means "transformations" or "changes." The author, Ovid, used ancient Greek myths as his principal subject matter and used the idea of changes as his leading motif—connecting the individual episodes within the poem.

Ovid was born as Publius Ovidius Naso in 43 B.C. in what is now central Italy. He died in Tomi, now Constanta, in A.D. 18.

His father, a landowner of some means, spared no expense in educating him; Ovid studied in Rome, and traveled over much of the Roman Empire to acquire knowledge. However, he refused to go along with his father's ambitions to make him into a public official. Instead, the young man devoted all his energies to the writing of poetry and became both rich and famous. He had a happy, amorous disposition and was for a while very popular with the "smart set" of Roman society. He married three times and became the father of a daughter.

Unfortunately for him, the mores of Roman society swung back to the puritanical ideals of an earlier age, frowning upon moral licentiousness both in public life and in literature. The Emperor, Augustus, spearheaded this change. At the very peak of his popularity and fame, Ovid invoked official censure and was sentenced to be banished to a desolate, faraway shore. The official charges against him were based on the supposed immorality of some of his poems, but public opinion held that there were other, unnamed reasons for the extreme severity of the sentence—perhaps a personal grievance of the Emperor. Ovid's third wife, who remained in Rome, championed his case loyally, but to no avail. He had to live out his life in Tomi, and die there, far from his beloved home, friends, and family.

His extant works—all but the *Metamorphoses* are written in elegiac couplets—fall into three principal groups. The *Amores* (*Loves*) traces a fictitious romance between the poet and a woman named Corinna—perhaps a composite of several of Ovid's lovers. The *Heroides* consists of imaginary letters written by famous women in literature and history, treating the female sex with sympathy and understanding, which was unusual in that age and culture. It also contains three pairs of correspondences between lovers. A book on makeup (a relevant aspect of the art of love) was followed by the notorious *Ars Amatoria* (*The Art of Love*, 1 B.C.) a handbook on seduction in three volumes, two for men and one for women.

From 1 B.C. onward, Ovid worked concurrently on his two masterpieces: the *Metamorphoses* and the *Fasti* (Roman religious holidays). The latter was planned to take the reader through the Roman calendar year, but he finished only the first six months at the time of his banishment. The work on which he hoped to base his claim to immortality, in any case, was the *Metamorphoses*, one of the world's supreme literary masterpieces.

After A.D. 9, the time of his exile, his main works were *Tristia* (*Sorrows*) and *Epistulae ex Ponto* (*Letters from the Black Sea*). To this day, they are the most consummate expressions of homesickness and pleading.

Historical Background

When Julius Caesar was murdered in 44 B.C., he had designated his adopted son and nephew, Gaius Octavius, his heir. The 18-year-old youth accepted the dangerous legacy and performed so well that his rule is generally considered one of the most glorious in Roman history and, perhaps, in all European history. Popularly known as Caesar Augustus, or "august Caesar," he was not only a great military leader but a superb administrator and a patron of the arts as well. During his reign, Roman literature came into its own, never to be surpassed in later ages. Among the authors who flourished in this, the Augustan Age, were Virgil, Horace, and Ovid.

Augustus was disturbed by the great moral laxity that had preceded his rule, and he was determined to put an end to it. It was this policy that destroyed Ovid's flourishing career in the capital, for, as he complained, "a poem and an error." Caesar, Augustus died in A.D. 14, but his successor, Tiberius, did not relent and Ovid was never permitted to return to Rome. With his death, the Golden Age of Roman literature came to an end.

Beginning with the two great poems attributed to Homer, the *Iliad and the Odyssey*, the epic has flourished in Western literature. Its main characteristics include an invocation to the Muse; a lofty subject matter; a dignified tone; a hero with a generally admirable character; a traditional subject matter; supernatural elements, and; so-called epic conventions, such as epic similes, catalogs of armies, etc. The traditional meter has been either the iambic hexameter (six scanning feet with one short syllable followed by a long one) or the distich (one hexameter line alternating with one iambic pentameter consisting of five iambic feet). The *Metamorphoses* follows some, but by no means all, of these conventions.

Metamorphoses is Ovid's only poem written in dactylic hexameters. It contains an Invocation of sorts: expressing a hope that the gods will help him. Its subject matter is traditional. It deals with ancient Greek myths and Roman traditions, but with a twist—the emphasis is on change. The idea that "everything always changes" was deeply imbedded in Greek thought starting with the philosopher Heraclitus, but Ovid transformed this dry philosophical tenet into dazzling poetry. He demonstrates that change is eternal and god-ordained, and that all life is interconnected.

The poem is full of supernatural elements; in fact, practically all of it concerns Greco-Roman divinities and their doings. However, unlike most other epic poems, it has no central hero—it ranges over the whole field of mythology, and its tone is, by turns, lofty or light, even flippant. Its main characters—depending on the interpretation the reader puts on the work—are either worthy of adoration (being gods and goddesses) or downright despicable, revealing their most un-godlike characteristics: jealousy, pride, envy, cruelty, petty rivalries. It is this tension, created by the contrast between the ostensibly divine characters and their less than admirable deeds, that gives the book its central momentum. This tension, together with Ovid's unsurpassable poetic gifts, has made the *Metamorphoses* a book universally admired in the poet's own age as well as through the centuries. The artists of the Renaissance used it as a veritable handbook for artistic themes. Among the innumerable poets who have read and enjoyed it, and borrowed copiously from it, are Chaucer and Shakespeare.

Master List of Characters

Book I

The poet—*Expresses intention to tell stories of transformations.*

Nature or God—*Force that put an end to original chaos.*

The Winds—*The winds that blow across the world's surface, including Zephyr god of the warm west, and Boreas, god of the cold the North Wind.*

Earth—*The planet whose land, air and water are ruled by the gods.*

Saturn—*Son of Heaven and Earth; father of three sons—Jove, Neptune, and Pluto; father of three daughters—Juno, Ceres and Vesta; father of Chiron the Centaur.*

Jove—*Lord of heaven; son of Saturn and Rhea, husband of Juno.*

Giants—*Attempted an attack on Heaven.*

Lycaon—*A barbarous king of Arcadia; turned into a wolf.*

Deucalion—*Son of Prometheus, husband of Pyrrha; spared from the primordial flood with his mate.*

Pyrrha—*Wife of Deucalion; spared from the flood with him, by order of Jove and attendant deities.*

Themis—*Goddess of justice, who hears the prayers of Deucalion and Pyrrha.*

Python—*A monstrous snake.*

Apollo (Phoebus)—*God of the sun, music, poetry, healing, archery and prophecy; sometimes known as Phoebus; father of Phaethon with Clymene; slays Python.*

Clymene—*Mother of Phaeton with Apollo; wife of Merops.*

Daphne—*First love of Apollo, daughter of the river god Peneus; turned into a laurel tree in answer to her prayer when she is pursued by Apollo; he takes her leaves for his emblem.*

Cupid—*God of love, in rivalry with Apollo.*

Diana (Artemis)—*Daughter of Jove and Latona; sister of Apollo; moon goddess and goddess of the hunt; patroness of young, unmarried women.*

Io—*Daughter of Inachus, worshipped also as Isis; desired by Jove; changed into a heifer; mother of Epaphus.*

Juno—*Queen of heaven, sister and wife of Jove; is well aware of his philandering ways.*

Argus—*Monster with 100 eyes who serves Juno; ordered to keep watch over Io.*

Mercury—*Messenger of the gods, son of Jove and Maia, takes pity on Io and slays Argus, enraging Juno.*

Syrinx—*Nymph chased by Pan, she is turned into a reed, from which he fashions his musical pipes.*

Phaethon—*Son of Apollo; friend of Epaphus, eager to prove his parentage; comes to grief driving his father's chariot of fire.*

Book II

Vulcan (Hephaestus in Greek)—*God of fire and metalworking; son of Juno, husband of Venus.*

The Sun-God—*Another name for Apollo or Phoebus; father of Phaethon with Clymene.*

Lucifer—*The morning star.*

Phaethusa and Lamperia—*Sisters of ill-fated Phaethon.*

Cygnus—*King of Liguria; turned into a swan and placed among the stars.*

Callisto—*An Arcadian nymph, seduced by love, and turned into a bear by Diana, goddess of the moon and the hunt. (She is not named here, but her story was known during Ovid's time.)*

Arcas—*Son of Caillisto, by Jove.*

Thetis—*A sea nymph, daughter of Neresu and Doris; wife of Peleus; mother of Achilles.*

Coronis of Larissa—*A nymph pursued by Apollo.*

Erichthonius—*A boy without a mother.*

Pallas Athena (also known as Athena or Minerva)—*Goddess of wisdom, craftsmanship and invention; daughter of Jove; patron goddess of Athens.*

Pandrosos, Herse and Aglouros—*Three sisters, daughters of Cecrops; the first two honorable, the third, not.*

Chiron—*An educated centaur; father of Ocyrhoe, by the nymph Chariclo.*

Ocyrhoe—*Daughter of Chiron; turned into a mare.*

Battus—*A roguish herdsman, turned to stone by Mercury for lying and cheating.*

Envy—*Green-fleshed monster whose tongue drips venom.*

Europa—*Abducted princess; daughter of Agenor; mother of Minos, the king of Crete.*

Book III

Agenor—*Father of the princess Europa, who is abducted; she becomes the mother of Minos, the king of Crete.*

Cadmus—*Son of Agenor; brother of Europa; defeats the dragon; founder of Thebes.*

Serpent—*Killed by Cadmus; the beast is sacred to Mars, god of War and son of Juno and Jove.*

Echion—*One of the survivors of a battle with troops who spring up from the serpents' teeth sown in the ground.*

Actaeon—*Hunter turned into a stag by the goddess Diana, after he sees her bathing; grandson of Cadmus.*

Semele—*Daughter of Cadmus; beloved of Jove; mother of Bacchus, the god of wine and ecstasy, who is also known as Dionysus.*

Dionysus—*Another name for Bacchus, the god of wine and ecstasy.*

Ino—*Sister of Semele, daughter of Cadmus, beloved of Jove, mother of Bacchus, the god of wine and ecstasy, who is also known as Dionysus.*

Tiresias—*Blind soothsayer whose gift of prophecy was given by Jove after his sight was taken as punishment by Juno; lived part of his life as a man and part of his life as a woman.*

Narcissus—*An unloving but beautiful and vain young man who breaks Echo's heart.*

Echo—*A nymph in love with Narcissus; she cannot speak except to repeat what others say.*

Nemesis—*Goddess of vengeance.*

Pentheus—*King of Thebes; son of Echion, who was one of the survivors of the battle with the troops sprung from dragon's teeth.*

Acoetes—*Devotee of Bacchus (Dionysus), the god of wine and ecstasy.*

Autonoe—*Aunt of Pentheus, the King of Thebes.*

Agave—*Mother of Pentheus, the Theban king.*

Book IV

Alcithoe—*A girl who, with her sisters, refuses to worship Bacchus, the god of wine and ecstasy (also known as Dionysus).*

Pyramus—*Lovers of Thisbe.*

Thisbe—*Babylonian girl, who is the lover of Pyramus.*

Leuconoe—*Sister of Alcithoe; tells the story of Mars and Venus.*

Mars and Venus—*Divine lovers, (the god of war and the goddess of love), they are snared by Vulcan's net.*

Leucothoe—*Daughter of Eurynome; dazzled, seduced and abandoned by Apollo, but still longing for him, then buried alive by her father.*

Eurynome—*Mother of Leucothoe.*

Clytie—*Enamored of Apollo, who despises her, she turns into a flower and daily turns to face the sun.*

Hermaphroditus—*Child of Hermes and Aphrodite (Mercury and Venus).*

Salmacis—*A naiad in love with Hermaphroditus.*

Minyas—*Father of Alcithoe and her sisters, who refuse to worship the god Bacchus (Dionysus).*

Athamas—*Husband of Ino, the daughter of Cadmus; brother-in-law of Semele.*

Cerberus—*Three-headed dog who guards the gates of the underworld.*

The Furies—*These three sisters—Alecto, Tisiphone, and Megaera, who are daughters of Uranus and Night—are the goddesses of vengeance; they also offer their protection at times.*

Tisiphone—*One of the Furies, she executes a command issued by Juno.*

Medusa—*One of the Gorgons, she was seduced by Neptune; Perseus slays her, and the sight of her severed head turns men to stone; drops of her blood turn into snakes; Pegasus, the enchanted flying horse, is also created from her blood.*

Perseus—*Slays the Medusa, by using his shield as a mirror for her; the sight of her severed head turned men to stone; he is the son of Jove and Danae.*

Atlas—*A giant who held the world on his shoulders; he is turned into a mountain by Perseus, who shows him the severed head of the Medusa.*

Andromeda—*A princess and the daughter of Cassiope and Cepheus, she is rescued by Perseus.*

Book V

Phineus—*Uncle of Andromeda and her promised husband.*

Cepheus—*Father of Andromeda, with Cassiope.*

Proteus—*A sea god.*

Polydectes—*Ruler of the tiny island of Seriphos; an antagonist of Perseus.*

Urania—*One of the nine Muses; daughter of Jove.*

Pegasus—*Enchanted horse who makes a stream appear on the land by striking his hoof on the ground; born from the blood of the Medusa.*

Pyreneus—*King of Thrace.*

Pierus and Euippe—*Their daughters opposed Minerva and became magpies.*

Thyphoeus—*A giant; a foe of the Olympian gods.*

Calliope—*Chief of the nine Muses, she is associated with epic poetry and songs; the steam-whistle musical instrument takes its name from her.*

Ceres (Demeter)—*One of the original, pre-Olympian divinities of the Mediterranean area; goddess of agriculture; sister-wife of Jove; mother of Proserpina (Persephone).*

Cupid (Eros)—*The god of love; son of Venus, the goddess of love.*

Pluto—*God of the underworld, the land of the dead; brother of Jove.*

Cyane—*A nymph who is turned into a pool.*

Arethusa—*A nymph who is turned into an underground river.*

Newt—*A loutish boy who is turned into a small reptile.*

Ascalaphus—*Turned into a screech owl for being a tattle-tale.*

Sirens—*Friends of Proserpina (Persephone)—turned into singing birds.*

Alpheus—*A river god who pursues Arethusa.*

Triptolemus—*Entrusted by Ceres to spread the cult of cereals.*

Lyncus—*Selfish king who is turned into a lynx.*

Book VI

Arachne—*Girl of humble origins whose weaving skills are masterly; she arouses the envy and anger of Pallas Athena and they compete to weave the most beautiful tapestry.*

Asterie, Leda, Alcmene, Danae, Aegina, Mnemosyne—*Women who were courted, seduced or raped by Jove; their stories are woven into a tapestry by Arachne.*

Melantho—*Ravaged by Neptune.*

Niobe—*Queen of Thebes, mother of many children, wife of Amphion; daughter of Dione and Tantalus; her children are slain because of her arrogance; she is turned into a stone by Jove.*

Latona (Leto)—*Mother of Apollo and Diana, with Jove.*

Marsyas—*A satyr who falls victim to Apollo's music-related jealousy.*

Tereus—*King of Thrace.*

Procne—*Wife of Tereus, daughter of Pandion, the king of Athens.*

Ithys—*Son of Procne and Tereus.*

Philomela—*Sister of Procne.*

Erechtheus—*Succeeds Pandion as king of Athens.*

Procris—*Daughter of Erechtheus; wed to Caphalus.*

Orithyia—*Daughter of Erechtheus; abducted by Boreas.*

Zetes and Calais—*Sons of Orithyia and Boreas; they become Argonauts.*

Book VII

Minyans (Minyae)—*An ancient, pre-Hellenic people whose domain is the starting point for the Argonauts, who are called the Minyae in the Metamorphoses.*

Phineus—*A Thracian king; a blind prophet tormented by harpies and rescued by the sons of Boreas (Different from the Phineus in Book V.)*

Harpies—*Monstrous birds with women's faces.*

Jason—*Leader of the Argonauts; son of Aeson.*

Phrixus—*Son of Athamas and Nephele; stepson of Ino; flees from stepmother's schemes with his sister, Helle, on a golden ram; arriving in Colchis, he sacrifices the ram and gives its golden fleece to King Aeetes, the father of Medea.*

Medea—*The daughter of King Aeetes; she is acquainted with magic and uses it on behalf of Jason, who seduces her.*

Hecate—*Goddess of enchantment and the world of night; she predates the Olympians.*

Aeson—*Deposed king of Thessaly; father of Jason.*

Aeacus—*One of the judeges of the underworld.*

Glaucus—*A fisherman who eats a magic herb and becomes a sea god pursues the nymph Scylla, who becomes a rock.*

Pelias—*Half-brother of Aeson; usurper of this throne.*

Cerambus—*Escapes the flood by being turned into a beetle.*

Aegeus—*King of Athens; father of Theseus.*

Theseus—*Celebrated hero of Athens; son of Aegeus.*

Minos—*King of Crete; son of Jove and Europa.*

Androgeos—*Son of Minos; treacherously slain in Athens during a contest.*

Book VIII

Nisus—*King of Megara; father of Nisus.*

Scylla—*Daughter of Nisus; betrays her father to ingratiate herself with King Minos; hanged into a bird.*

Daedalus—*Athenian inventor and architect; father of Icarus; dreams of flight lead to tragedy.*

Icarus—*Son of Daedalus; participates in father's dreams of flight with tragic results.*

Ariadne—*A princess of Crete.*

Minotaur—*A monster, half-man and half-bull, who resides on Crete.*

Meleager—*Son of Oeneus, king of Calydon, and Althaea; becomes an Argonaut.*

Castor and Pollux—*Twin brothers who become constellations; sons of Leda, who was raped by Jove.*

Atalanta—*A young woman from Arcadia, she is a champion hunter and a warrior.*

Plexippus and Toxeus—*Uncles of Meleager.*

Althaea—*Mother of Meleager; sister of Plexippus and Toxeus.*

Deianira and Gorge—*Sisters of Meleager.*

Oeneus—*Putative father of Meleager.*

Achelous—*A river god.*

Pirithous and Lelex—*Hunters who are Meleager's fellow woodsmen.*

Philomen and Baucis—*A pious old couple.*

Erysichthon—*A king who offends Ceres.*

Mestra—*Daughter of Erysichthon; she is not named in the story, but Ovid's contemporaries knew who she was.*

Book IX

Hercules—*A celebrated hero. known for his strength; son of Jove with Alcmena.*

Nessus—*A centaur in love with Deinaira.*

Iole—*A princess captured by Hercules.*

Lichas—*A servant of Deinaira.*

Geryon, Cerberus, Hydra, etc.—*Victims of Hercules during his Twelve Labors.*

Philoctetes—*Son of Poeas; friend of Hercules.*

Eurystheus—*King of Mycenae; at Juno's command, imposes the Twelve Labors on Hercules.*

Hyllus—*son of Hercules.*

Ilithyia (Lucina)—*Goddess of childbirth.*

Galanthis—*Servant girl of Alcmena.*

Dryope—*Half-sister of Alcmena; mother of Amphissus with Apollo; married by Andraemon.*

Lotis—*A naiad, pursued by Priapus, the god of gardens and vineyards.*

Iolaus—*Nephew and companion of Hercules; when Hercules asks Hebe, Iolaus is rejuvenated.*

Hebe—*Daughter of Juno; given to Hercules as a wife after he is made a god.*

Capaneus—*Argive chief; one of the Seven Against Thebes.*

Callirhoe—*Gains special grace from Jove.*

Iasion—*Beloved by Ceres.*

Anchises—*Mortal father of Aeneas.*

Aeacus—*Son of Jove by Aegina.*

Radamanthus—*One of the judges of the underworld, with Minos and Aeacus; a son of Jove.*

Miletus—*A son of Apollo and Deione.*

Maeander—*A river turning on itself.*

Cyane—*A nymph changed by Pluto into a pool.*

Caunus and Byblis—*Children of Cyane and Miletus.*

Ops—*Ancient deity; wife of Saturn in Roman beliefs.*

Thetys—*Wife of Ocean in the pre-Olympian times; not to be confused with Thetis, a sea nymph who is the wife of Peleus and the mother of Achilles.*

Sons of Aeolus—*Certain of these men committed incest with their sisters.*

Ligdus and Telethusa—*Parents of Iphis.*

Inachus—*Father of Io; after she flees to Egypt, she becomes a manifestation of the goddess Isis.*

Anubis, Bubastis Apis, Harpocrates, Osiris—*Ancient Egyptian divinities whose history had reached the Roman empire when Ovid was writing.*

Ianthe—*Daughter of Teleses, chosen by Ligdus as a wife for Iphis.*

Hymen—*The god of marriage.*

Book X

Orpheus—*A great musician; son of the muse Calliope.*

Ixion, Tityos, and the Daughters of Belus—*Sufferers in the underworld—the world of the dead.*

Eurydice—*Wife of Orpheus.*

Pluto (Hades)—*God of the world of the dead, called the underworld or Dis.*

Charon—*Boatmen whose cargo is the souls of the dead.*

Attis—*A beautiful shepherd beloved by the goddess Cybele.*

Cyparissus—*A handsome young man believed to have been invented by Ovid.*

Ganymede—*A beautiful boy abducted by Jove to be a cupbearer.*

Hyacinthus—*Believed of Apollo; probably pre-dates the Olympic pantheon.*

Propoetides—*Formerly sacred women of Cyprus.*

Pygmalion—*A Cyparian who made a statue of a young woman and fell in love with it.*

Galatea—*The transformation name given to the statue.*

Paphos—*The daughter of Pygmalion and Galatea.*

Cinyras—*The son of Paphos.*

Myrrha—*The daughter of Cinyras.*

Cencheris—*The wife of Cinyras.*

Adonis—*Beloved by Venus; son of Myrrha and her father, Cinyras.*

Hippomenes—*In love with the swift young woman Atalanta.*

Book XI

Midas—*King of Phrygia; known for his lack of taste, judgment and wisdom; be careful what you wish for because you might get it.*

Silenus—*A satyr; foster father of Bacchus (Dionysus), the god of wine and ecstasty.*

Eumolphus—*Singer; priest of Ceres.*

Pan—*The god of the woods and of shepherds.*

Laomedon—*King of Troy; father of Priam.*

Hesione—*A Trojan princess.*

Thetis—*A sea nymph; mother of Achilles.*

Ceyx—*King of Trachis; husband of Alcyone.*

Daedalion—*Brother of Ceyx; father of Chione.*

Chione—*Daughter of Daedalion; pursued by Apollo and Mercury; bore Philammon and Autolycus.*

Oneton—*A herdsman of Peleus.*

Acastus—*King of Magnesia.*

Morpheus—*Son of Somnus; the god of sleep.*

Aesacus—*Half brother of Hector.*

Hesperie—*A nymph, beloved of Aesacus.*

Book XII

Priam—*The last king of Troy.*

Hector—*Priam's most valiant son.*

Paris—*Another son of Priam; his abduction of Helen leads to the Trojan War.*

Calchas—*An interpreter of dreams.*

Nereus—*A sea god or the sea itself.*

Agamemnon—*King of Mycanae; leader of the Greek forces against Troy.*

Iphigenia—*Daughter of Agamemnon.*

Protesilaus—*First victim of the war.*

Cygnus—*One of several heroes with the same name; each is changed into a swan.*

Menoetes—*A victim of Achilles.*

Nestor—*King of Pylos.*

Caeneus—*Born a girl, Caenis, and changed into a male; invinvible hero.*

Ixion—*King of the Lapithae; ancestor of the centaurs by a cloud.*

Pirithous—*Son of Ixion with a mortal mother.*

Hippodame—*Wife of Pirithous.*

Eurytus—*A wild centaur.*

Many of the Lapithae and centaurs—*Killed in the melee caused by Eurytus.*

Cyllarus—*A handsome centaur in love with Hylonome.*

Tiepolemus—*Son of Hercules.*

Diomedes—*Greek hero.*

Ajax the Lesser—*Son of Oileus; Greek hero.*

Menelaus—*King of Sparta; husband of Helen; brother of Agamemnon.*

Ulysses and Ajax the Greater—*Contenders for the armor of Achilles.*

Book XIII

Palamedes—*Greek warrior who tells tales about Ulysses and is cleverly betrayed by him.*

Philoctetes—*Friend of Hercules; heir to his bow and arrows.*

Rhesus—*Thracian king; prevened from reaching Troy by Ulysses.*

Dolon—*A Phrygian spy slain by Ulysses.*

Helenus—*Son of Priam with the gift of augury; captured by Ulysses.*

Diomedes—*King of Argos; frequent companion of Ulysses.*

Pyrrhus—*Son of Achilles; his mother is a princess of Scyros, where Achilles was hidden to prevent him from going to war.*

Teucer—*Half-brother of Ajax; cousin of Achilles.*

Telephus—*Wounded then cured by Achilles.*

Antenor—*Trojan chief, ready with Priam to return Helen to the Greeks.*

Thersites—*A mean man; chastised by Ulysses.*

Sarpedon—*Son of Jove and Europa; cut down by Patroclus; harried by Ulysses.*

Alastor, Chromius, Coeranos, Alcander, etc.—*Victims of Ulysses.*

Patroclus—*Friend of Achilles who wears his armor; drives back Trojans but is slain by Hector.*

Pleiades—*Daughters of Atlas; a constellation represented on the shield of Achilles.*

Orion—*A celebrated constellation.*

Eurypylus, Thoas, Meriones—*Greek captains.*

Cassandra—*Trojan princess whose prophecies are not believed.*

Astyanax—*Infant son of Hector; hurled from the battlements of Troy.*

Trojan women—*Abducted by the Greeks as the spoils of war.*

Hecuba—*Queen of Troy; after the death of her last child, she turns into a dog and flees.*

Polydorus—*A Trojan prince, sent by Priam to Thrace, and treacherously slain there.*

Polymester—*A greedy ruler; murders Polydorus.*

Polyxena—*Youngest daughter of Hecuba; sacrificed to the hose of Achilles.*

Aurora—*Goddess of the dawn; mother of Memnon, a Trojan ally.*

Aeneas—*Son of the goddess venus by Anchises; a Trojan prince.*

Ascanlus—*Young son of Aeneas.*

Anius—*Priest of Apollo at Delphi.*

Therses—*A guest of Anius.*

Scylla—*Now incarnated as a dangerous monster; later becomes a rock.*

Charybdis—*A nymph; also a dangerous whirlpool opposite Scylla the rock.*

Galatea—*A sea nymph, lover of Acis, pursued by the Cyclops Polyphemus.*

Acis—*Lover of Galatea; killed by Polyphemus; turned into a river.*

Glaucus—*Formerly a fisherman, now a river god; loves Scylla but is loved by Circe.*

Circe—*An enchantress; falls in love with Glaucus, is rejected by him and punishes his beloved Scylla.*

Oceanus and Tethys—*Titans who are ancestors of some of the gods.*

Triton—*A sea god.*

Book XIV

Dido—*Queen of Carthage.*

Acestes—*A Sicilian king of Trojan descent.*

Iris—*Messenger of Juno.*

Sibyl (Sibylla)—*Priestess of Apollo at his temple.*

Caieta—*Old nurse of Aeneas.*

Macareus—*Companion of Ulysses.*

Achaemenides—*Companion of Ulysses.*

Aeolus—*King of the winds.*

Antiphates—*King of the Lestrygonians.*

Polites, Eurylochus and Elpenor—*Messengers of Ulysses to Circe.*

Cyllenius—*Mercury; named after his birthplace.*

Picus—*Son of Saturn, a local god.*

Canens—*A nymph loved by Picus.*

Turnus—*A king of the Rutuli in Italy, and a rival of Aeneas for Lavinia's hand.*

Evander (Euander)—*An ally of Aeneas.*

Venulus—*A messenger sent by Turnus to Diomedes.*

Acmon—*Companion of Diomedes; changed into a bird by Venus.*

Iulus—*Another name for Ascanius, the son of Aeneas.*

Indiges—*The name under which the deified Aeneas was worshipped.*

Silvius, Latinus, Alba, Epytus, Capys, Capetus, Tiberinus—*Rulers after Iulus.*

Acrota—*Son of Tibernus.*

Romulus—*Son of Mars; founder of Rome.*

Aventinus and Procas—*Famous rulers.*

Pomona and Vertumnus—*Native deities of growth and fertility.*

Iphis—*A young man of common origins who is in love with the princess Anaxarete.*

Numitos—*A Roman king.*

Ausonia—*Italy.*

Amulius—*Son of Numitor; deposes his father; is deposed by Romulus.*

Pales—*Goddess of herds.*

Tatius—*Sabine king who warred with Romulus but later shares power with him.*

Tarpeia—*Roman maid who opened the gates to the Sabines and is killed by them.*

Cures—*A Sabine city.*

Ilia (Rhea Sylvia)—*Daughter of Numitor; mother of Romulus with Mars.*

Quirinus—*The name Romulus carries after his apotheosis.*

Hersilia—*Widow of Pomulus; known as Hora after her apotheosis.*

Book XV

Numa—*King of Rome after Quirinis.*

Croton—*Hero who entertained Hercules; namesake of Crotona.*

Myscelus—*Founder of Crotona.*

Pythagoras—*Greek philosopher; born in Samos and migrated to Crotona.*

Euphorbus—*A brave Trojan who is killed.*

Helenus—*Advises Aeneas about the future.*

Thyestes—*Brother of Atreus—fed on the flesh of his sons.*

Egeria—*Wife of Numa.*

Hippolytus—*Son of Theseus and the Ammazon Hippolyta; tells his story to Egeria.*

Phaedra—*Stepmother of Theseus.*

Paeon—*Son of Apollo; inherits the god's healing power and applies it to Aesculapius.*

Virbius—*The name by whick Hippolytus is known after his rebirth.*

Tages—*A deity sprung from a clod.*

Cipus—*A Roman who refused the kingship.*

Aesculapius (Asclepius; Imhotep)—*Son of Apollo, god of healing.*

Caesar—*Family name of Julius Caesar; presumably descended from Iulus, the son of eneas.*

Caesar Augustus—*Adopted son and heir of Julius Caesar.*

Vesta—*Goddess of hearth and home.*

Summary of the Poem

Ovid himself sums up his poetic intention in the introductory quatrain (four-line unit) of the *Metamorphoses:*

> My intention is to tell of bodies changed
> To different forms; the gods, who made the changes,
> Will help me — or I hope so — with a poem
> That runs from the world's beginning to our own days.

These few lines explain that he will sing about changes: that the changes were brought about by the gods; and that he will sing a continuous song, encompassing tales from the creation of the world to his own time. Accordingly, the poem begins with the first change—when God or Nature ended the original chaos, separating land from water and sky, and the denser air from the light, fiery ether of the stratosphere. From that modest beginning, the Earth globe, the winds, stars, beasts, and mankind, evolved. History itself may be divided into four periods: the Golden Age, the Age of Silver, (and with it the four seasons), the Age of Bronze, and the Age of Iron, including the present.

When mankind became violent and wicked, Jupiter destroyed the world with the Flood; but the goddess Themis arranged a second creation by means of changing stones to people. A particularly vicious man, Lycaon, had already been turned into a wolf. A pattern had been established.

Almost imperceptibly, Ovid shifts from the story of the second creation into his main narrative: how the Earth had brought forth Python, a monstrous serpent; how Apollo killed Python with his arrow, founded the sacred Pythian games, and ordained that the winners should be crowned with oak leaves because the laurel of later victories did not yet exist. From this casual mention of the laurel, the poem moves effortlessly to the story of how the laurel came into being, the story of Apollo and Daphne. Daphne became the innocent victim of a wanton contest between Apollo and Cupid. To prove that even Apollo may be wounded by Cupid, the young god of love shoots an arrow into Apollo which causes him to become obsessed with desire for Daphne. Daphne is shot by another arrow which drives all love away. In a desperate flight to avoid Apollo's unwanted advances, Daphne seeks divine intervention and is turned into a laurel tree.

This account of innocent maidens fleeing the rapaciousness of male gods is one of the typical story lines in the *Metamorphoses*, but the variations on it are endless. They explain how nymphs were turned into birds, flowers, reeds, and stones; how certain stars were placed into the Heavens; how the younger generation of gods and demigods came into being. The poem flows along almost like a stream, and it carries the reader with it.

More careful reading, however, reveals that this apparently seamless garment is artfully constructed. While it appears to be a chronological account of world history, certain pieces are placed out of chronological order into a thematic scheme. Toward the end, when the poem is already recounting the early history of Rome and approaching the poet's own times, the undoing of the city of Croton seems to be included mainly to give occasion to introduce the teachings of Pythagoras, a Greek philosopher and mathematician, who, as a refugee from his native island, came to Croton and taught the citizens there. By setting forth the revolutionary thoughts of Pythagoras, (relative to vegetarianism and reincarnation), Ovid departs from tales of mythical gods and goddesses to champion Pythagoras' causes. So eloquent is he in showing the evils of killing animals for food that all his arguments could have been written by modern-day vegetarians. But then Ovid skillfully returns to his narratives—King Numa, successor to Romulus, had listened to the teachings of Pythagoras! After Numa's death, his wife Egeria mourns for him so piteously that she is scolded by Theseus' son Hippolytus. This, in turn, provides an opportunity for Ovid to introduce the story of Hippolytus a young man, an innocent victim of slander, who was brought back from death, proving Pythagoras' thesis of the immortality of the soul and the indestructibility of matter. With the threat of his banishment hanging over him, Ovid hastened to bring his tale up to date, ending with the deification of Julius Caesar, Augustus' adopted father. He announced confidently that the work will endure and that the immortal part of himself, his soul, will survive.

Estimated Reading Time

The poem is divided into fifteen Books. Allowing two to three hours per book, the student should be able to read the entire *Metamorphoses* in 30 to 45 hours.

SECTION TWO

The Metamorphoses of Ovid

Book I

New Characters:

The poet: *expresses intention to tell stories of transformations*

Nature or God: *force that put an end to original chaos*

The Winds: *the winds that blow across the world's surface, including Zephyr god of the warm west, and Boreas, god of the cold the North Wind*

Earth: *the planet whose land, air and water are ruled by the gods*

Saturn: *son of Heaven and Earth; father of three sons—Jove, Neptune, and Pluto; father of three daughters—Juno, Ceres and Vesta; father of Chiron the Centaur*

Jove: *lord of heaven; son of Saturn and Rhea, husband of Juno.*

Giants: *attempted an attack on Heaven*

Lycaon: *a barbarous king of Arcadia; turned into a wolf*

Deucalion: *son of Prometheus, husband of Pyrrha; spared from the primordial flood with his mate*

Pyrrha: *wife of Deucalion; spared from the flood with him, by order of Jove and attendant deities*

Themis: *goddess of justice, who hears the prayers of Deucalion and Pyrrha*

Python: *a monstrous snake*

Apollo (Phoebus): *god of the sun, music, poetry, healing, archery and prophecy; sometimes known as Phoebus; father of Phaethon with Clymene; slays Python*

Clymene: *mother of Phaeton with Apollo; wife of Merops*

Daphne: *first love of Apollo, daughter of the river god Peneus; turned into a laurel tree in answer to her prayer when she is pursued by Apollo; he takes her leaves for his emblem*

Cupid: *god of love, in rivalry with Apollo*

Diana (Artemis): *daughter of Jove and Latona; sister of Apollo; moon goddess and goddess of the hunt; patroness of young, unmarried women*

Io: *daughter of Inachus, worshipped also as Isis; desired by Jove; changed into a heifer; mother of Epaphus*

Juno: *queen of heaven, sister and wife of Jove; is well aware of his philandering ways*

Argus: *monster with 100 eyes who serves Juno; ordered to keep watch over Io*

Mercury: *messenger of the gods, son of Jove and Maia, takes pity on Io and slays Argus, enraging Juno*

Syrinx: *nymph chased by Pan, she is turned into a reed, from which he fashions his musical pipes*

Phaethon: *son of Apollo; friend of Epaphus, eager to prove his parentage*

Summary

The poet expresses his intention to tell the stories of changes of bodies to different forms, since the beginning of the world to the present time. He hopes that the gods will aid him in this endeavor, since it was they who made those changes.

In the beginning, there was Chaos, inert, shapeless matter. Eventually, either God or Nature began creation by separating different elements out of the confusion—Heaven, Earth, water, land, air, ether. This same Creator formed Earth and made it into a great globe, floating in water; five climatic zones were established

as well as rivers, lakes, and warring winds, stars in the heavens, fish, beasts, and birds. The last being to be added was Man, in God's image, (or Earth's with a divine spark), looking toward Heaven.

The Golden Age was perfect. None of the later banes of civilization existed: no law, no punishment, no judges; no ships, no towns, no armies; no agriculture. Men were happy. Then, after the murder of Saturn by Jove, the Age of Silver came into existence. The four seasons were established, and houses and agriculture were introduced. The Age of Bronze brought on aggressive instincts; men were quick to arm, but were not yet evil. The Iron Age let loose all evil. The "damned desire of having" induced people to all kinds of violence and crimes. Shipfaring began, trees were cut down, and the land once the common property of all was divided up into parcels. War, murder, and plunder spread until Justice, the last of the immortals, deserted the earth. Heaven was no safer. Giants attacked Heaven and had to be defeated.

As Jove was witness to these atrocities, he remembered an experience he had with a wicked man, Lycaon, who outraged the principles of hospitality by offering him, Jove, human flesh to eat, and also by planning to kill him. Jove punished him by turning him into a wolf. He called a divine council and suggested that all mankind, being evil, should be destroyed by a flood. The gods agreed, and all living beings were destroyed, except one pious couple. When Deucalion and Pyrrha realized that they were the only survivors, they prayed to the goddess Themis who granted them the ability to recreate mankind from stones. However, some of the new creation, too, was undesirable, such as the monstrous serpent, Python, which was then killed by Apollo.

Apollo fell in love with Daphne, daughter of a river-god. This passion was the work of Cupid, whom Apollo mocked. Cupid shot Apollo with a love-inducing arrow, and Daphne with a love-repelling one. In a desperate attempt to evade Apollo's unwanted advances, Daphne implored the river-god Peneus to save her. She was turned into a laurel tree.

A similar transformation happened to another maiden, Io. Jove ravished her, but his wife, Juno, discovered his cheating. Trying to evade her wrath, Jove changed Io into a beautiful white cow. Juno slyly demanded that he hand over the cow to her. Unwilling to

betray himself, he did so. The unfortunate girl was put into the custody of the hundred-eyed giant, Argus, who treated her cruelly. She was able to reveal her identity to her father, but he could not help her and grieved bitterly. Finally, Jove sent his son Mercury to kill Argus. Mercury accomplished this task by putting Argus to sleep by telling a story of another metamorphosis. This was the tale of the nymph Syrinx. This nymph was pursued by the god Pan and was turned into a group of reeds. Eventually, all of Argus' hundred eyes were closed in slumber, and Mercury dispatched him with a blade. Juno pursued the pitiable Io all the way into Africa. Jove begged for Juno's forgiveness, and she relented, allowing Io, gradually, to change back into her human form. The girl gave birth to a son, Epaphus, the seed of Jove. His companion was Phaethon, son of Apollo.

Epaphus insulted his friend by suggesting that Phaethon's mother, Clymene, may have been lying about his parentage. Clymene encouraged the young demigod to go see his father in far-away India, and the youth delightedly undertook the journey.

Analysis

What is the meaning of these myths and the others that will follow? Throughout the ages, they have been told and retold, depicted in art, even set to music. Are they simply figments of the imagination?

The reader should be aware of the fact that there is a branch of learning, mythography, and that there have been and still are numerous schools of thought about the origin and meaning of myths.

For a long time, it was believed that all myths arose to explain to "primitive men" the world around them: the sun, the moon, the stars, etc., and the gods were "fashioned" to satisfy some primitive urge to worship powers greater than themselves. This theory has only a limited application, once we leave the areas of cosmogony, the creation story itself, (the "nature myth" theory). The story of the Great Flood could be explained by observing that it occurred in the mythologies of nearly all races and that it probably recorded an actual event in the prehistoric memory of mankind. But what about the numerous myths about the Voyages of the Argonauts and the

Trojan War? Archeological research has proven that these events had actually happened, while the details in them need to be carefully evaluated and interpreted, (the "myth as history" approach).

Similarly, the myth of the crimes of Lycaon and their fierce punishment may help codify ancient taboos concerning lack of hospitality, cannibalism, and murder. It also warns the reader against *hubris*, arrogant pride, for Lycaon wanted to test the god's omniscience and power.

What about the myths dealing with the gods and their often unsavory acts? Could such capricious, unpredictable, unreasonable, cruel beings ever have been sincerely worshipped? Or were they simply symbols, abstractions invented to deal with the frightening puzzle of existence? This theory could be labeled the "metaphysical approach."

In the years immediately preceding Ovid's own career, some of the tales became the vehicles of patriotic propaganda, as in Virgil's great *Aeneid*, building a support system for the Roman Empire. Toward the end of the *Metamorphoses*, Ovid follows Virgil's example. Did he truly believe that Romulus, or his wife Hersilia, or Julius Caesar actually became gods and that Caesar Augustus was on the road to becoming a god? Some scholars find it difficult to believe this. Did Ovid write these passages because he sensed that he needed to seek favor with the puritanical Emperor? It is an open question. On the other hand, the sophisticated Ovid, while never convincing us that he believed in the literal existence of the gods and nymphs he depicts, made their stories into supreme entertainment, appealing to the whole gamut of emotions. What more heartrending story than that of the innocent Io and her futile attempts to communicate with her father? What suspense as the reader follows her flight through two continents!

There are several more scholarly approaches to mythography. Some Freudians view the myths of the rapes of nymphs as expressions of the horror some virgins have of the sexual act. Others, Robert Graves in particular, show painstakingly that, "A large part of Greek myths is politico-religious history. All early myths about the gods' seduction of nymphs refer apparently to marriages between Hellenic chieftains and local Moon-priestesses; bitterly opposed by Hera (Juno), which means by conservative religious feeling." He explains the myth of Apollo's destruction of the Python at Delphi and the attempted rape of Daphne as a "true myth," recording the Achaeans' (early Hellenic tribes') capture of the Cretan Earth-goddess' shrine, the establishment of the Pythian Games at Delphi, and the cult of Daphne's sacred grove, which survived into historical times. Graves devoted two books to this subject—his two-volume *The Greek Myths,* and *The White Goddess.* They give interesting and informative backgrounds to the reading of the *Metamorphoses.*

Study Questions

1. How did Ovid modify the traditional Invocation to the Muse?

2. Who or what changed the original Chaos into the World we now have?

3. What was the form that the Earth took?

4. What were the Four Ages, and what were their characteristics?

5. What was the cause of the Flood?

6. What were the sins of Lycaon, and how was he punished?

7. Who or what was Python, and what was its fate?

8. What was the origin of the laurel tree?

9. Daphne, Io, and Syrinx have a common thread in their tales. What is it?

10. What was the taunt of Epaphus aimed at Phaethon? What was its result?

Answers

1. He simply expressed his intention to tell the stories with the possible help of the gods.

2. The change was the work of Nature or God.

3. Earth was a globe, not a flat disk as later "experts" claimed.

4. The Four Ages were: the Age of Gold, perfection; the Age of Silver, still very good, but with the coming of the seasons bringing extremes of heat and cold; the Age of Bronze, in which weapons were introduced; and finally, the Age of Iron,

during which every evil was loosed upon the world. (Ovid adapted this theory from the Greek poet Hesiod.)

5. Jove saw the wickedness of mankind and persuaded the other gods to punish it.

6. Lyacon planned to murder Jove in his sleep (an extreme example of lack of hospitality); he also tried to feed him human flesh (cannibalism). He was also guilty of *hubris*, testing Jove's omniscience and power.

7. Python was a monstrous serpent, a by-product of the second creation. Apollo killed the serpent with his arrows.

8. As Daphne was fleeing Apollo, Diana changed her into a laurel tree. Apollo then made the laurel the badge of victory in the Pythian Games, an antecedent of the Olympic Games.

9. All three maidens were pursued by gods who wanted to rape them.

10. Epaphus challenged Phaethon to prove that his mother was not a liar and that he was truly the son of the Sun-god.

Suggested Essay Topics

1. Book I of the *Metamorphoses* presents numerous similarities to the Judeo-Christian traditions of the Creation and the early history of mankind. What are some of them?

2. There are many contrasts between the Greek traditions and the Judeo-Christian traditions. What are some of them? Specifically, comment on the different conceptions of divinity. What are some of the characteristics of Graeco-Roman gods which set them apart from the Judeo-Christian conception of God?

Book II

New Characters:

Vulcan (Hephaestus in Greek): *god of fire and metalworking; son of Juno, husband of Venus*

The Sun-God: *another name for Apollo or Phoebus; father of Phaethon with Clymene*

Lucifer: *the morning star*

Phaethusa and Lamperia: *sisters of ill-fated Phaethon*

Cygnus: *king of Liguria; turned into a swan and placed among the stars*

Callisto: *an Arcadian nymph, seduced by love, and turned into a bear by Diana, goddess of the moon and goddess of the hunt. (She is not named here, but her story was known during Ovid's time.)*

Arcas: *son of Caillisto, by Jove*

Thetis: *a sea nymph, daughter of Neresu and Doris; wife of Peleus; mother of Achilles*

Coronis of Larissa: *a nymph pursued by Apollo*

Erichthonius: *a boy without a mother*

Pallas Athena (also known as Athena or Minerva): *goddess of wisdom, craftsmanship and invention; daughter of Jove; patron goddess of Athens*

Pandrosos, Herse and Aglouros: *three sisters, daughters of Cecrops; the first two honorable, the third, not*

Chiron: *an educated centaur; father of Ocyrhoe, by the nymph Chariclo*

Ocyrhoe: *daughter of Chiron; turned into a mare*

Battus: *a roguish herdsman, turned to stone by Mercury for lying and cheating*

Envy: *green-fleshed monster whose tongue drips venom*

Europa: *abducted princess; daughter of Agenor; mother of Minos, the king of Crete*

Summary

Phaethon visited his father, the Sun-god Apollo, who received him warmly and offered him anything he wished. The young man rashly demanded the opportunity to drive the Sun's chariot for one day. Apollo regretted his promise but could not go back on it. Phaethon had a disastrous ride and soon lost control of the horses, falling headlong through the skies. Everything in his path burned, and the conflagration threatened the whole Earth. Jove killed him with a thunderbolt. His mother and sisters mourned him; the girls were turned into trees. Cygnus, a relative, became a swan. Afterward, Jove visited Arcady, and became enamored with a nymph, Callisto. Jove approached her in the guise of the goddess Diana, and seduced her, making her pregnant. The goddess herself banished the girl from her circle of virgin huntresses, and Juno, ever jealous, turned her into a bear. Her child, Arcas, out hunting, almost killed her, but Jove intervened and turned both mother and son into constellations, the Big Bear and the Little Bear.

The story of how the raven, once white, became black illustrates the consequences of gossiping. Apollo's bird, the raven, wanted to report to his master that he saw Coronis, a girl Apollo had seduced, with another lover. The crow tried to dissuade the raven, by relating a story of her own gossiping which was not appreciated by the Goddess Minerva. The daughters of Cecrops were entrusted by Minerva with safekeeping a boy born without a mother, Erichthonius, under strict orders not to pry into the chest which contained him. One of the daughters, Aglauros, defied the prohibition and undid the fastenings. The crow reported it to the goddess but, instead of receiving thanks, was demoted. The crow mentions that she, too, was a beautiful girl once, was ravished by the god of the ocean and was turned into a bird by Minerva as a way of escape, but now Nyctimene, "another sinful woman," has become Minerva's favorite, the owl.

The raven did not heed the warning and reported the affair of Coronis to Apollo. The angry god killed the girl with an arrow. When the dying girl reported that by killing her he had also killed her child, Apollo rescued the child and entrusted it to the centaur, Chiron. He hated the raven for having told him that the girl had another lover, and caused him to become black.

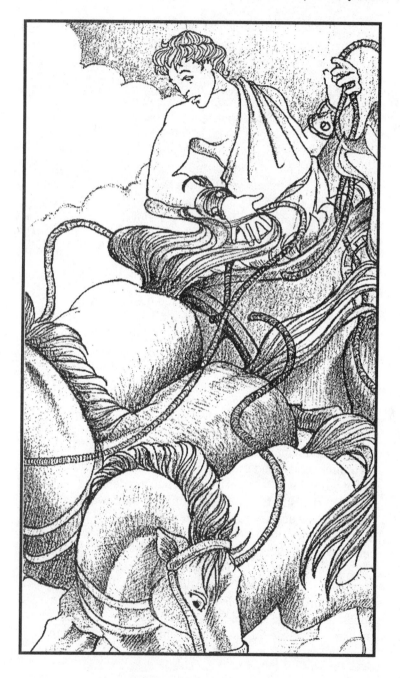

Chiron's daughter Ocychroe predicted the fate of Chiron and her own child and was punished by being turned into a horse. Apollo could not save her; he was away, playing music. His cattle wandered off and Mercury stole them. The theft was witnessed by a servant, Battus. Mercury bribed him but then tricked Battus and turned him into a stone.

Next, Mercury lusted after Cecrops' middle daughter, Herse, and tried to bribe the eldest girl, Aglauros, into admitting him into Herse's room. Aglauros accepted the bribe, but Minerva, still angry at Aglauros for having peeped at the concealed child Erichthonius, exacted a punishment. She visited the goddess Envy and ordered her to kill Aglauros. Envy carried out the command and inflicted a horrible disease on Aglauros who eventually turned into black marble. Mercury, too, was satisfied that the greedy girl was punished and flew off to Heaven.

Mercury was given another errand by his father Jove to steal some cattle in Sidon. That accomplished, Jove disguised himself as a bull and seduced the king's daughter, Europa, carrying her across the sea.

Analysis

Book Two begins with the story of Phaethon, son of Apollo. As an illustration of the consequences of arrogant behavior (*hubris*) in a young man, it has been employed as a story with a moral. As a nature-myth, it seems to record the prehistoric memory of a giant comet which caused a catastrophic conflagration and whose smoke even blacked out the light of the sun. Some scientists now believe that a similar cosmic catastrophe may have led to the extinction of the dinosaurs, millions of years earlier. Ovid is at his best in describing this gigantic event. The metamorphoses of Phaethon's sisters and cousin, by contrast, seem gratuitous and unmotivated either in a moral or a scientific context and appear to record some ancient folk-tales whose origins are now lost to us. Ovid took his materials wherever he found them and was satisfied to create a rich tapestry of them.

"The Story of the Raven, and the Raven's Story" demonstrates Ovid's playful technique of telling a tale within the tale, with its seemingly whimsical moral: to "Keep out of trouble and be quiet!" It is sadly ironic that Ovid's own banishment could probably have been avoided had he followed his own advice; there is reason to believe that he knew about some scandals in the family of Augustus that the emperor wished to suppress, and Ovid committed some "error" of indiscretion.

This whole group of stories shows the consequences of inappropriate behavior and overstepping one's bounds, a form of violation of *moira*. Gossiping to a superior or even telling the truth in the hopes of currying favor does not work and is often dangerous. Another form of indiscretion is illustrated in the myth of the "boy born without a mother." The child was a protégé of the goddess Minerva, herself supposedly "born without a mother." The goddess, by her Greek name Athena Parthenos, was the patron deity of the city-state of Athens; the city was anxious to perpetuate her reputation as a virgin, symbolic of the invincibility of their state. Her fierce protection of the boy is nowhere explained in the poem, but it is difficult to avoid the suspicion that she herself was the boy's mother; the gossips said she was raped by Vulcan. (On the Acropolis of Athens, next to Athena's own temple, the most beautiful edifice is the Erechtheion; Robert Graves suggests that *Erechtheus*, the name of one of Athens' first kings, may be an alternate way of referring to Erechthonius.) Whatever the reason for the secrecy, Minerva punished the indiscretion of Aglauros horribly.

In addition to further rapes and seductions by Jove, Apollo, and Neptune, in this book the character of Mercury is elaborated upon: he is now shown to be a god of thieves as well.

Study Questions

1. What was the central imagery of the artwork on the gate on the Palace of the Sun?

2. Who or what were the companions of the Sun-god sitting on his throne?

3. Why did Phaethon ask for his fatal ride, and why did his father permit it?

4. Why is the Tiber, a small river, included in the list of great rivers?

5. How did the "almighty father" terminate the catastrophe of Phaethon's folly?

6. Why did Jove descend to Arcady?

7. What is the significance of the fact that Callisto and Arcas must be "kept out of the water?"

8. How is Apollo's grief over Coronis different from human grief?

9. What is the irony of the fate of the goddess Envy?

10. What were the transgressions of Aglauros?

Answers

1. Vulcan decorated it with images of the sea and creatures inhabiting the sea.

2. The god was attended by Days, Months, Years, Centuries, Hours, and Seasons.

3. The son was guilty of *hubris*, arrogant pride, imagining himself in the same class as his divine father; the father agreed out of overly permissive love.

4. The city of Rome, where Ovid and the emperor live, is on the Tiber.

5. Jove hurled his thunderbolt.

6. The god came to Arcady to assess the damage done by Phaethon's disastrous fall and the fire which resulted.

7. The constellations of the Big Bear and Little Bear never set in the sea.

8. Gods cannot weep.

9. Envy's successes are self-defeating; in hurting a mortal, she pleases a goddess.

10. She was guilty of disobedience and indiscretion, prying into Minerva's secret, looking at the "boy without a mother." She was also greedy and envious of her sister.

Suggested Essay Topics

1. In several of the tales of seduction and/or rape by a god, the victim gets blamed, called ugly names, and punished or at

least abandoned. Comment on this attitude of "blaming the victim" in the light of attitudes toward rape victims today.

2. Which of the myths in this book may be used to illustrate: a) nature myths; b) moral instruction; c) politico-religious history?

Book III

New Characters:

Agenor: *father of the princess Europa, who is abducted; she becomes the mother of Minos, the king of Crete*

Cadmus: *son of Agenor; brother of Europa; defeats the dragon; founds Thebes*

Serpent: *killed by Cadmus; the beast is sacred to Mars, god of War and son of Juno and Jove*

Echion: *one of the survivors of a battle with troops who spring up from serpents' teeth sown in the ground*

Actaeon: *hunter turned into a stag by the goddess Diana, after he sees her bathing; grandson of Cadmus*

Semele: *daughter of Cadmus; beloved of Jove; mother of Bacchus, the god of wine and ecstasy, who is also known as Dionysus*

Dionysus: *another name for Bacchus, the god of wine and ecstasy*

Ino: *sister of Semele, daughter of Cadmus, beloved of Jove, mother of Bacchus, the god of wine and ecstasy, who is also known as Dionysus*

Tiresias: *blind soothsayer whose gift of prophecy was given by Jove after his sight was taken as punishment by Juno; lived part of his life as a man and part of his life as a woman*

Narcissus: *an unloving but beautiful and vain young man who breaks Echo's heart*

Echo: *a nymph in love with Narcissus; she cannot speak except to repeat what others say*

Nemesis: *goddess of vengeance*

Pentheus: *king of Thebes; son of Echion, who was one of the survivors of the battle with the troops sprung from dragon's teeth*

Acoetes: *devotee of Bacchus (Dionysus), the god of wine and ecstasy*

Autonoe: *aunt of Pentheus, the King of Thebes*

Agave: *mother of Pentheus, the Theban king*

Summary

Jove and Europa arrived in Crete. Her father, Agenor, sent his son Cadmus in search of her. Afraid to return without her, Cadmus sought and found a new homeland but had to battle a monstrous serpent in a cave. After killing the serpent, he received divine instruction to sow its teeth. He obeyed and a race of armed men arose. They fought each other until only five survived. One of those was called Echion. He and his brothers helped Cadmus build the city of Thebes. Cadmus and his wife were happy, but the poet issues the traditional warning: "Call no man happy until his burial."

In the story of Cadmus' grandson, Actaeon, the poet addresses the reader: "You will find Actaeon guiltless; put the blame on luck, not crime: what crime is there in error?" The young man happened to see Diana naked and was turned by her into a stag; his own bloodhounds tore him to pieces. Juno rejoiced in the disaster of Agenor's household. "All of Europa's relatives were guilty, because Europa had been Junos' rival." Now she had a new grievance because Semele, daughter of Cadmus, was pregnant by Jove. (The Queen of Heaven uses quite undignified, slangy language, referring to the affair as a "hole-and-corner business.") This time, instead of cursing Jove, she decided to employ trickery. Disguising herself as Semele's servant, she persuaded the young woman to challenge Jove to reveal himself to her in his full divine majesty. Jove, sorrowfully, did so; Semele was consumed by fire. The child in her womb was saved, however. Jove sewed it up in his own thigh until it came to term. Semele's sister Io cared for the infant.

In a happier mood, Jove and Juno argued about who had more pleasure in sex, men or women. Jove maintained that women did; Juno disagreed. They called on Tiresias to decide, for he had been both man and woman in his lifetime. Tiresias gave his vote to Jove; Juno, angered, struck him blind. Jove softened the blow by giving him power to foretell the future.

Tiresias foretold that Narcissus, a beautiful boy, would live to an old age, "if he never knows himself." Pursued by the nymph Echo, he rudely rejected her; Echo wasted away until only her voice remained. Another spurned lover cursed him to suffer from unrequited love. Nemesis, Goddess of Vengeance, made the vain youth fall in love with his own reflection in a pool. Unable to satisfy his desire to embrace the image, Narcissus pined away. In place of his body, the mourners found "nothing, except a flower with a yellow center surrounded with white petals."

Tiresias was honored for his prophetic powers, but Pentheus, Echion's son and King of Thebes, scorned him and mocked his blindness. The prophet predicted that the king would come to a horrible end once Bacchus came to Thebes. Indeed, Pentheus forbade the worship of the new god and declared war on him. Acoetes, a devotee of Bacchus, was arrested and testified to the power of the god who had saved him from a terrible predicament. Pentheus was unconvinced and went to the mountain where the worshippers of Bacchus were celebrating his secret rites. In a sacred frenzy, even his aunt and mother failed to recognize him and tore him to pieces.

Analysis

This book centers around the transformations in the House of Cadmus, brother of Europa. Juno, in her jealousy and hatred of Europa, persecutes her whole family: her brother Cadmus, his grandson Actaeon, sister Semele (a new lover of Jove and therefore a new offense to her dignity). In the next book, her wrath will extend to Ino, Semele's sister and her husband, both of whom are innocent, good people, their only offenses being that they are related to Semele and are happy. Actaeon's offense is clearly an error, yet, his punishment is vicious. (Ovid, too, was claiming that one of the reasons for his banishment was an error, but his punishment, too, was carried out without mercy.) Many ancient people, the Greeks among them, believed that to behold a god merited death. In that spirit, Actaeon had to die; the same held for Semele. Yet, the gods had their own "code" also: once a god made a promise, he had to keep it, even if the results were unfortunate for the person who extracted the promise. Similar ancient taboos survive in the fates

of those who are over-confident, arrogant, or too sure of their happiness. Taunting or scorning those who are less fortunate than oneself, old or blind persons, for instance, was also considered wrong and was punished. Finally, this book shows that all gods must be accepted on faith. Pentheus was destroyed chiefly because he refused to worship Dionysus/Bacchus.

Study Questions

1. Which god is Cadmus attempting to honor when he sends his men into the forest?

2. Which god does he unintentionally offend?

3. Cite an obvious overstatement in the description of the serpent.

4. What prophecy does Cadmus hear after killing the serpent?

5. What was the name of the city founded by Cadmus?

6. Is it believable that the dogs would not have recognized their master, even if metamorphosed?

7. Characterize Jove's behavior toward Semele before and after her destruction.

8. What is the meaning of Tiresias' answer regarding Narcissus' future?

9. Narcissus gave his name not only to a flower but to a psychological problem as well. What does it mean when a person is characterized as "narcissistic?"

10. What was the result of Pentheus' death in the City of Thebes?

Answers

1. He wishes to honor Jove.

2. He offends Mars, to whom the serpent (some call it a dragon) is sacred.

3. It is said to have been as huge "as the great serpent of the constellations," with the whole world beneath him.

4. He is told that he, too, will some day be a serpent.

5. The city of Cadmus and his descendants was Thebes.

6. It is difficult to believe that dogs would not recognize their master, no matter what; Ovid and his readers would have known that. This is an example which shows that these myths were intended to be symbolic and poetic, not realistic or factual.

7. While Semele was his lover, he tried to please her by promising to fulfill her wish, and even swore on the River Styx that he would do so. After her death, he went on relaxing and joking with his wife, Juno.

8. Tiresias' riddling answer means that Narcissus will have a long life only if he never knows himself: he must not see his image either physically or emotionally—not know how beautiful and desirable he is.

9. A person is characterized as "narcissistic" when he or she becomes overly proud of some personal trait such as beauty, attractiveness, and, by extension, accomplishments, intelligence, etc., and treats others with disdain.

10. After the Thebans saw what happened to Pentheus, they thronged to the altars of Bacchus.

Suggested Essay Topics

1. Juno's hatred and jealousy of Europa and Semele eventually extended to all of their relatives and even the whole community of Thebes. How do you feel about this concept of collective guilt or "guilt by association?" Are there examples of this concept still alive today?

2. Serpents are mentioned several times in this Book. Give examples of the many roles they play in the lives of the characters. Compare them with modern attitudes toward serpents.

Book IV

New Characters:

Alcithoe: *a girl who, with her sisters, refuses to worship Bacchus, the god of wine and ecstasy (also known as Dionysus)*

Pyramus: *lovers of Thisbe*

Thisbe: *Babylonian girl, who is the lover of Pyramus*

Leuconoe: *sister of Alcithoe; tells the story of Mars and Venus*

Mars and Venus: *divine lovers, (the god of war and the goddess of love), they are snared by Vulcan's net*

Leucothoe: *daughter of Eurynome; dazzled, seduced and abandoned by Apollo, but still longing for him, then buried alive by her father*

Eurynome: *mother of Leucothoe*

Clytie: *enamored of Apollo, who despises her, she turns into a flower and daily turns to face the sun*

Hermaphroditus: *child of Hermes and Aphrodite (Mercury and Venus)*

Salmacis: *a naiad in love with Hermaphroditus*

Minyas: *father of Alcithoe and her sisters, who refuse to worship the god Bacchus (Dionysus)*

Athamas: *husband of Ino, the daughter of Cadmus; brother-in-law of Semele*

Cerberus: *three-headed dog who guards the gates of the underworld*

The Furies: *these three sisters—Alecto, Tisiphone, and Megaera, who are daughters of Uranus and Night—are the goddesses of vengeance; they also offer their protection at times*

Tisiphone: *one of the Furies, she executes a command issued by Juno*

Medusa: *one of the Gorgons, she was seduced by Neptune; Perseus slays her, and the sight of her severed head turns men to stone; drops of her blood turn into snakes; Pegasus, the enchanted flying horse, is also created from her blood*

Perseus: *slays the Medusa, by using his shield as a mirror for her; the sight of her severed head turned men to stone; he is the son of Jove and Danae*

Atlas: *a giant who held the world on his shoulders; he is turned into a mountain by Perseus, who shows him the severed head of the Medusa*

Andromeda: *a princess and the daughter of Cassiope and Cepheus, she is rescued by Perseus*

Summary

Pentheus was not the only person to refuse to worship Bacchus. The daughters of Minyas were guilty as well. On holidays ordained by Bacchus, they continued to work on their weaving, spinning, and needlework, keeping their serving-women by them, also. One of these women, a great storyteller, entertained them with numerous tales. The story of Pyramus and Thisbe related the tragic deaths of two true lovers. Leuconoe, one of Minyas' daughters, repeated the well-known story of how Vulcan trapped his unfaithful wife, Venus, in a cunning chain fashioned by him while she was making love to Mars. The spy who had reported the lovers was the Sun-god himself, and Venus punished him through his current love, Leucothoe. Jealous Clytie reported the affair to her rival's father who buried Leucothoe alive. The Sun-god could not revive Leucothoe but turned her into a fragrant shrub, frankincense. Clytie was metamorphosed into a sunflower, forever turning after her faithless lover, in vain.

Alcithoe then related the story of Salmacis, a fountain which makes men weak. The child of Mercury and Venus, Hermaphroditus, was pursued by a water-nymph but rejected her. She embraced him passionately, "as a serpent / Caught by an eagle, borne aloft, entangles / Coils around head and talons, or as ivy / Winds round great oaks, or an octopus extends / Its prey within its tentacles." In despair, he asked for a curse on the pool.

The daughters of Minyas were punished by Bacchus by being turned into bats. By now Bacchus was universally acclaimed. His aunt, Ino, was especially proud of him. However, Juno was still offended that any member of her rivals' families should prosper.

She descended to Dis, or Hades, saw the famous sinners of antiquity being punished there, and ordered one of the Furies to destroy the happiness of Ino and her family. Her command was executed in a most horrible fashion: Ino and her good husband Athamas were made insane and killed their own children. Venus took pity on them and, with the help of Neptune, turned them into divinities. The Theban women, however, mourning them, were changed into rocks and sea-birds.

Cadmus and his wife did not know that Venus had intervened on behalf of their children. In their sorrow, they turned into gentle serpents and went into hiding.

Bacchus, worshipped in India as well as in Greece, ascended Olympus. Only the king of Argos still resisted him and another child of Jove, Perseus. Fresh from having defeated the snake-headed monster Medusa, this offspring of Jove and Danae flew through the air, dropping snakes from Medusa's hair over Lybia, driving through space, north and south, east and west, finally landing near the giant, Atlas, possessor of a tree with golden apples. Because of an ancient oracle, Atlas distrusted Perseus' offer of friendship, whereupon Perseus showed him Medusa's head, instantly turning Atlas into a mountain. Next, he flew to Ethiopia. From the air, he saw the beautiful Andromeda who was chained, naked, to a rock, an innocent victim of the boasting of her mother about her beauty. The god Ammon punished her in this cruel way, setting a monster to guard her. Her parents, standing nearby, were grieving, which "struck Perseus / As pretty futile." He obtained the parents' consent to marry Andromeda should he be able to free her. His victory over the monster was due not only to superhuman strength and agility but also a clever trick. He attacked it from the air, like an eagle, and the monster mistook Perseus' reflection on the water for the hero himself. Next, Perseus buried Medusa's head for protection, built three altars, and married Andromeda. During the festivities, he related to his new parents-in-law how he had slain Medusa. He also told them that Medusa had once been a beautiful girl, but Neptune had ravished her in Minerva's temple, and the goddess, "punishing the outrage / As it deserved," changed the girl's hair to snakes.

Analysis

The priests of Bacchus ordained that on the festivals of the god all work should cease. The daughters of Minyas disobeyed and had to be punished. It did not help them that, in continuing their accustomed labors, they had been serving Pallas. The stories they told while working give a good indication of how the ancient myths were passed on by word of mouth. Some of them were so well known that Ovid refers to them only in passing; some, like that of Pyramus and Thisbe, he elaborates on. This story of true love opposed by parents and ending in the death of the lovers impressed Shakespeare, inspiring the plot of *Romeo and Juliet*: he also burlesqued it by the comical manner in which it is performed by the "mechanicals" in *A Midsummer Night's Dream*. In Ovid's version, the myth explains why the fruit of the mulberry tree turns from white to blood-red.

The story of Mars and Venus, lifted straight from Homer, is used to introduce the myth of the Sun-god and Leucothoe. According to Robert Graves, in the more ancient versions of that myth, the Sun-god is not Apollo but the more ancient Helius, son of a titaness by Jove; his affair with Leucothoe, whose name means "White Goddess," reflects one of the stages by which Sun-worship gradually replaced Moon-worship in the Mediterranean.

Alcithoe probably said the truth when she declared that the story of Hermaphrodite was new. It was the kind of story Ovid's contemporaries would have appreciated, with its effeminate men and aggressive women. The myth of the fate of Minyas' daughters and the gory story of the destruction of Ino and her family, however, take the tale back to ancient horrors of the curse on the House of Cadmus and the City of Thebes. Juno's descent into Hell represents one of the most ancient myths recorded in history: on the tablets of Sumer, about 3000 B.C., Inanna, Queen of Heaven, descends to the Nether World; since that time, nearly every epic hero has imitated her, including Odysseus-Ulysses and Aeneas, to mention just two. There is a bittersweet ending to the saga of Cadmus and his kin—he started his career by defeating a serpent and ended up becoming a serpent himself. This fact is ironic, but also symbolic if we consider that the serpent is often depicted as biting its own tail—a circle returning to itself.

A deft transition is made to the next cycle of narratives, those concerning Perseus, the eponymous hero of Persia. Some aspects of it were so well known that Ovid takes them for granted: how he defeated the Gorgon Medusa, and the fact that everyone looking at her—or her head, even after Perseus cut it off—was instantly turned into stone. He also omits mentioning that the reason Perseus was able to fly was that Mercury loaned him his winged sandals. Accounting for the multitude of serpents in Libya, he also relates the origin of the Atlas Mountains, of coral beds, and recounts the sad tale of how a beautiful girl was turned into a monster as a "punishment" for having been raped.

Study Questions

1. Was the taboo against working on holidays a Greek specialty? What other religious traditions have similar prohibitions?

2. Book Four illustrates one of the manners in which myths have come down through ancient times. What was it?

3. How did women in ancient Greece occupy themselves?

4. What metamorphosis is explained by the myth of Pyramus and Thisbe?

5. What aspects of that myth did Shakespeare "borrow" for *Romeo and Juliet*?

6. In what way did he employ the same source in *A Midsummer Night's Dream*?

7. In many ancient societies, and in some societies even today, the punishment for a woman caught in adultery is instant death. How is the gods' code different for the same offense, as shown by the treatment of Venus when caught in a net with Mars?

8. In what new role do we see Clytie in this book?

9. With all the tales of rapacious male gods, how does Ovid show that passionate pursuit is not a male prerogative?

10. What figure of speech is employed to characterize the attack of the monster on Perseus?

Answers

1. Most religions have a taboo against working on a holiday, for example, Jews are not supposed to work on the Sabbath, Christians on Sunday, Muslims on Friday.

2. While women did their spinning, weaving, and needle-working, one of them entertained the others with stories.

3. Women spun thread, wove cloth, and sewed garments and other necessities for themselves and others.

4. The mulberry tree's fruit is white when unripe but turns red later.

5. In *Romeo and Juliet*, a young couple is kept apart by unreasonable parents; accidents and misunderstandings cause them to kill themselves, but their parents later regret their harsh treatment of them.

6. Shakespeare makes the tragic tale comical through the use of bungling actors and bizarre adaptations of the story line.

7. Instead of being punished with death, Venus shrugs off the incident, and the gods have a good laugh at the expense of the lovers, as well as of the cuckolded husband.

8. Clytie, fond mother of Phaethon in Book One, is now a jilted and jealous lover, causing her rival's death.

9. The water-nymph Salmacis pursues and seduces Hermaphroditus.

10. The monster is compared to a galley bearing down on its target. The figure of speech is a simile.

Suggested Essay Topics

1. In each book, Ovid introduced us to more and more of Jove's far-flung offspring. If we accept Graves' theory of the symbolic meaning of these "rapes" and the resulting offspring, how do these myths show the expansion of the patriarchal system with its primacy of the worship of the sun over the older matriarchal system and its moon-worship? Be specific by identifying some of the geographical designations found in the poem. (For example, Europa is taken by Jove from Sidon to Crete. Trace this on the map.)

2. This book, more than the previous ones, employs casual, colloquial speech. Give examples and discuss whether in your opinion they are appropriate to the speaker and situation or not, and why.

Book V

New Characters:

Phineus: *uncle of Andromeda and her promised husband*

Cepheus: *father of Andromeda, with Cassiope*

Proteus: *a sea god*

Polydectes: *ruler of the tiny island of Seriphos; an antagonist of Perseus*

Urania: *one of the nine Muses; daughter of Jove*

Pegasus: *enchanted horse who makes a stream appear on the land by striking his hoof on the ground; born from the blood of the Medusa*

Pyreneus: *king of Thrace*

Pierus and Euippe: *their daughters opposed Minerva and became magpies*

Thyphoeus: *a giant; a foe of the Olympian gods*

Calliope: *chief of the nine Muses, she is associated with epic poetry and songs; the steam-whistle musical instrument takes its name from her*

Ceres (Demeter): *one of the original, pre-Olympian divinities of the Mediterranean area; goddess of agriculture; sister-wife of Jove; mother of Proserpina (Persephone)*

Cupid (Eros): *the god of love; son of Venus, the goddess of love*

Pluto: *god of the underworld, the land of the dead; brother of Jove*

Cyane: *a nymph who is turned into a pool*

Arethusa: *a nymph who is turned into an underground river*

Newt: *a loutish boy who is turned into a small reptile*

Ascalaphus: *turned into a screech owl for being a tattle-tale*

Sirens: *friends of Proserpina (Persephone)—turned into singing birds*

Alpheus: *a river god who pursues Arethusa*

Triptolemus: *entrusted by Ceres to spread the cult of cereals*

Lyncus: *selfish king who is turned into a lynx*

Summary

The wedding feast of Perseus and Andromeda was rudely interrupted by her uncle, Phineus, on the grounds that she had been promised to him. Cepheus, the girl's father, argued that without Perseus the girl would now be dead, but Phineus hurled his spear at Perseus. Perseus counterattacked and missed, hitting someone else. From that point on, the festivities turned into a hideous free-for-all, and untold casualties resulted.

Greatly outnumbered, Perseus could not have survived, had it not been for the timely appearance of his half-sister Minerva who gave him her shield and reassurance. The epic battle ended with Phineus and his surviving allies being turned to stone when Perseus contrived to have them look at the Gorgon Medusa. Returning home a victor with his bride, Perseus had to reclaim his ancestral city from usurpers, a task he also accomplished with the help of the Medusa.

Minerva now flew to Thebes, to Hilicon where the Muses lived. She asked her half-sisters to show her the new fountain sprung under the hoof of the winged horse, Pegasus, born from the blood of the Medusa. The sisters mentioned their fear of the likes of the Thraciacan king Pyreneus who had earlier threatened them with violence. Their conversation was interrupted by nine magpies; one of the muses told their story.

The magpies used to be women, but they committed an offense against the muses by boastfully challenging them to a singing contest. The first of them launched into a mocking song about the Olympian gods. The muse then asked whether Minerva would like to hear what their response had been. Reassured, the muse related what the muses' contribution had been: it was the story of Ceres, inventor of agriculture, giver of laws.

Pluto, king of the underworld, came to Earth. Venus, irritated by the fact that Pluto had not yet acknowledged her powers, incited her son, Cupid, to shoot his love-arrow into the king. Ceres' virgin daughter, Proserpina, was gathering flowers when Pluto "took her" in a "rush of love." After ravishing her, he also kidnapped her in his chariot. The nymph Cyane tried to stop him but was turned into a pool. Ceres, searching for her daughter, tired and thirsty, stopped at a peasant hut to ask for water. The old woman who lived there gave her a cup of water sweetened with barley kernels. Her loutish son mocked Ceres as she greedily drank. Angry, Ceres threw the contents of the cup on him. He turned into a spotted lizard-like creature, a newt.

Eventually, Ceres discovered the truth: her daughter had been taken to the world below. In her grief, she cursed the land of Sicily and destroyed its fertility. Another nymph, Arethusa, arose from the pool she lived in and described to Ceres what had happened to Proserpina. Ceres drove her chariot to Heaven and demanded justice from her husband-brother, Jove. The king of the gods tried to defend his brother; Proserpina's return was also blocked by the Fates who had determined that, once she had eaten anything in the underworld, she must remain there. A witness said that Proserpina had indeed eaten seven seeds of a pomegranate. Ceres, enraged, turned the tattler into a screech-owl. Proserpina's faithful companions, who had helped search for her, were also turned into birds: they are the Sirens, birds with a sweet voice and women's faces, forever scanning the sea.

In the end, Jove worked out a compromise. Proserpina must spend part of the year with her husband, but during the rest of the year she may return to Earth to be with her mother. Ceres, mollified, returned to Arethusa to hear the story of that nymph. It, too, turned out to be a story of a woman trying to escape the unwanted advances of a male; she succeeded only by becoming an underground river, running from Arcadia in central Greece to Sicily.

Now Ceres flew in her chariot to Athens, where she gave Triptolemus some grain with instructions to spread its cultivation abroad. He was successful in Europe, and in part of Asia, up to the land of the Scythians, but king Lyncus tried to take credit for the benefits for himself. He was turned into a lynx.

The muses had decided that the contest had ended in their favor and, when the competitors demurred, turned them into chattering birds.

Analysis

The sharply divided Book Five shows two widely differing talents of Ovid. In the first part he upholds the epic tradition of a great battle scene with scores of individual victims named and each dying in different, spectacular, and often gory ways. That done, he uses the figure of Minerva, whose contributions to the battle had been quite vague, to transfer the scene to the charming environment in which the Muses abide. While acknowledging that even in Helicon a female's privacy may be invaded, he introduces, among others, the important myth of Ceres and Proserpina. This is done "Chinese-box-style": an unnamed Muse relates what the chief Muse, Calliope, had said earlier.

The myth of Ceres and Proserpina (Demeter and Persephone) is among the oldest in the Mediterranean area. Ceres was the original culture-heroine: she gave mankind laws and grains, the means to survive. (Our word 'cereal' derives from her name.) In the mythical birth-order of the gods, she is older than Jove, showing that her worship was more ancient than his. With the enthronement of the Olympians, she had to be "married" to one of them, of course, but she was accepted as one of their own. This myth helped to explain, in an era much more naive and unsophisticated than Ovid's, the alternation between fertile and infertile seasons of the year. By his time, several subsidiary myths had been attached to it: the origins of the lynx, the newt, the sirens, and a chattering bird which may not have been the same as the one referred here as a magpie. Ovid, as always, added some touches of his own.

Study Questions

1. Who was the first person to disturb the festivities at the wedding of Perseus and Andromeda?

2. What was the reason for the provocation?

3. What did Andromeda's father point out?

4. Describe the fates of Athis and Lycabas.

5. How did Perseus dispatch Erytus?

6. Were there any neutrals present? What happened to them?

7. How did Perseus finally defeat Phineus?

8. Describe the treachery of Pyreneus.

9. Name some geographic terms that are "explained" by incidents in this Book.

10. What is peculiar in the way in which the Muses conduct their contest?

Answers

1. Phineus, brother of Andromeda's father, disturbed the festivities.

2. He claimed that Andromeda had been promised to him. (This detail was added by Ovid.)

3. Cepheus pointed out that, without Perseus, the girl would now be dead.

4. The two boys, dear companions, were brutally slain by Perseus.

5. Perseus hit Erytus over the head with a large mixing-bowl.

6. Several would-be neutrals were also killed.

7. Perseus finally turned Phineus into stone by forcing him to look at Medusa.

8. Pyreneus offered protection to the Muses and then attacked them sexually.

9. To mention just a few: the Pyrenees, Arethusa, Cyane, Mt. Etna, and Sicily.

10. They act as contestants, judges, jury, and executioners of the punishment.

Suggested Essay Topics

1. Comment on Perseus' behavior during his wedding "festivi-
    ties." Granted that Phineus attacked him first, can you justify
    the savagery of his subsequent deeds? Note especially the
    fates of the innocent bystanders. Comment also on his be-
    havior immediately following his victory.

2. The song of the woman who turned into a magpie gives an
    interesting twist to the characterization of the Olympian
    gods. Analyze the text by comparing each "portrait" to the
    orthodox image of each divinity. What does this section tell
    you about Ovid's own belief in the Olympians?

Book VI

New Characters:

Arachne: *girl of humble origins whose weaving skills are masterly;
she arouses the envy and anger of Pallas Athena and they
compete to weave the most beautiful tapestry*

Asterie, Leda, Alcmene, Danae, Aegina, Mnemosyne: *women who
were courted, seduced or raped by Jove; their stories are woven
into a tapestry by Arachne*

Melantho: *ravaged by Neptune*

Niobe: *queen of Thebes, mother of many children, wife of Amphion;
daughter of Dione and Tantalus; her children are slain because
of her arrogance; she is turned into a stone by Jove*

Latona (Leto): *mother of Apollo and Diana, with Jove*

Marsyas: *a satyr who falls victim to Apollo's music-related jealousy*

Tereus: *king of Thrace*

Procne: *wife of Tereus, daughter of Pandion, the king of Athens*

Ithys: *son of Procne and Tereus*

Philomela: *sister of Procne*

Erechtheus: *succeeds Pandion as king of Athens*

Procris: *daughter of Erechtheus; wed to Caphalus*

Orithyia: *daughter of Erechtheus; abducted by Boreas*

Zetes and Calais: *sons of Orithyia and Boreas; they become Argonauts*

Summary

Hearing the story told by the Muses, Minerva decided to punish someone who had offended her by boasting. She was thinking of a girl who, though of humble origins, claimed to be a better weaver than Minerva herself. The goddess, disguising herself as an old woman, warned Arachne against being overly proud and impious, but the girl refused to listen. Even when Minerva revealed herself in her divine splendor, Arachne insisted on a contest. Both of them produced masterpieces. Minerva's tapestry represented her victory over Neptune for patronage of the city of Athens; it also showed other scenes illustrating the folly of mortals' competing with divinities. She "signed" it with a border of a peaceful olive-wreath.

Arachne's subject was the deceitful way in which gods dealt with mortal girls. She showed a whole list of Jove's rapacious dealings with women; she also included other gods in her tableau. When Minerva realized that Arachne's work was as faultless as her own, she became furious; she battered the girl savagely. Arachne, in despair, tried to hang herself. Minerva "took pity on her" and let her live, but metamorphosed her into an ugly spider which "has not forgotten / The arts she used to practice."

A woman who had been a girlhood acquaintance of Arachne was now Queen Niobe. She and her husband both had divine antecedents; in addition, she could boast of an extraordinary family of seven sons and seven daughters. Her tragic mistake was that she "thought herself the happiest of all mothers." In her foolish pride she offended Latona, the nymph who bore the twins Apollo and Diana to Jove. Latona exacted a terrible vengeance on Niobe. Summoning her divine children, she ordered them to kill all of Niobe's family with their arrows. In her overwhelming grief, Niobe turned to stone. Niobe's fate reminded all who heard of it of similar incidents involving gods and boasting mortals. One of the tales, that of Apollo's vengeance on the satyr Marsyas, was particularly horrible.

The neighboring rulers all sent condolences to Niobe's

country, Thebes, except for Athens, which was suffering from a barbarian invasion. Tereus, king of Thrace, sent an army to aid Athens. In gratitude, he received the daughter of Pandion, king of Athens, as wife. In spite of bad omens, Tereus and Procne were married and soon had a son, Ithys.

Five years later, Procne petitioned her husband to bring her sister Philomela for a visit. Tereus agreed and sailed to bring Philomela to Procne. But when he saw Philomela, lovely and beautiful, Tereus was overcome with an insane passion for her. After obtaining her father's permission, he sailed for home with his sister-in-law, but, upon reaching dry land, took her to an abandoned building and ravished her brutally. The girl, desolated, gave him a furious tongue-lashing, threatening to reveal his crime to her sister. The cruel king cut out her tongue and raped her again and again. He left her in the abandoned building and made up some lie about her absence.

Philomela managed to send a message to her sister who swore a terrible vengeance. Taking advantage of a ritual orgy in honor of Bacchus, she sought out her sister, disguised her, and brought her home. Trying to punish her husband, she slaughtered their young son Ithys and served him to Tereus in a dish. It was Philomela who hurled the bloody head of Ithys full in his father's face. The sisters then flew from his fury, turned into birds, and he, too, metamorphosed into one: a hoopoe.

Old Pandion went into a swift decline; his throne went to Erechtheus, who had several children. One of his daughters was courted by Boreas, who came from the homeland of Tereus. His suit was refused, but he took the girl anyway. They settled in Athens and eventually had two sons, Zetes and Calais, who later became Argonauts.

Analysis

This book is linked to the preceding one by the theme of "contest." Minerva, usually a beneficent deity, here becomes vengeful and punishes a mortal woman who has no other offense but a great gift, her beautiful weaving, and the fateful flaw of pride. Minerva's famous art of the disguise is also displayed. Ovid is at his best in developing a slight folk-tale into a dazzling performance of a contest between two master-weavers. Each woman chooses a topic appropriate to her own personality and world-view. Arachne's cloth shows, in miniature, much of the subject-matter of the first three books of the *Metamorphoses*. The fact that Ovid dares to present the gods in such a manner, without being afraid of the gods' vengeance, is one of the best indications that, for him, these gods are already dead.

The story of Niobe is one of the best-known myths. It has tremendous pathos and has become the subject of a famous Hellenistic statue, presently in the Uffizi Gallery in Florence, Italy. The story contains one of the most fundamental tenets of Greek thought, that one must not tempt the gods by boasting of luck or good fortune or happiness, for they can be lost instantly. Niobe was the happiest of mothers, but, because she thought of herself as such, she was made into the unhappiest of mothers. There is tremendous irony in the fact that her tragedy is caused by none other than Latona, who had herself been the victim of cruel persecution by Juno. In this case the "contest" occurs not between a god and a mortal but between two mortal women with divine family ties.

It is at this point that the poem itself undergoes a pivotal change of direction. The classical scholar, William S. Anderson, points out that the theme of mortals challenging gods and being punished trails off at line 6.400 of Book Six, then "makes a slow but obvious transition to a totally different kind of story, whose complex themes are human lust, brutality, and bloody vengeance within families." The metamorphoses of that unhappy trio, Tereus, Procne, and Philomela, are not the works of the gods but the results of the lust and brutality of Tereus and the bloody vengeance of Procne and Philomela. These passions occur within a human, not a divine, family. Ovid will continue along similar lines, marking one of the two major dividing lines in the poem.

Study Questions

1. What new traits of Minerva are displayed in this Book?

2. What fatal error does Arachne commit when visited by Minerva in disguise?

3. What is the insurmountable difference, therefore, between gods and mortals?

4. What was the common theme of the design in the corners of Minerva's canvas?

5. What was the common theme running through Arachne's work?

6. What was the irony of the motif that Minerva chose for the border of her work?

7. What was the irony of Niobe's boast of her ancestors?

8. What was the response of the people to Latona's vengeance?

9. What is peculiar about the response everyone, including the victim, expresses with respect to the rape of Philomela?

10. What distinguishes the metamorphoses of Tereus, Procne, and Philomela from the previous ones?

Answers

1. Minerva is arrogant, deceitful, and cruel.

2. Arachne is stubborn and overly proud; she is guilty of *hubris*.

3. Gods and mortals are not equal and mortals forget this fact at their own peril.

4. All four corners shouted "Danger!" at overly bold individuals.

5. Arachne depicted the misdeeds of gods.

6. It was ironic that Minerva used the olive, symbol of peace, in a canvas that was a not-so-concealed threat at Arachne.

7. Niobe's ancestors, especially the Titans, Tantalus, and Atlas, were themselves punished by the Olympian gods.

8. The people reminded themselves that the gods must be feared.

9. It is peculiar that everyone, including Procne and Philomela herself, acted as though the victim had been somehow to blame for what happened.

10. In the case of these three people, we are not told that a god effected the transformation; it just "happened."

Suggested Essay Topics

1. If you compare this book with the earliest ones, do you find an increasing complexity of characterization? Give examples.

2. This Book is especially rich in figures of speech, particularly extended similes. Give examples.

Book VII

New Characters:

Minyans (Minyae): *An ancient, pre-Hellenic people whose domain is the starting point for the Argonauts, who are called the Minyae in the Metamorphoses*

Phineus: *a Thracian king; a blind prophet tormented by harpies and rescued by the sons of Boreas (different from the Phineus in Book V.)*

Harpies: *monstrous birds with women's faces*

Jason: *leader of the Argonauts; son of Aeson*

Phrixus: *son of Athamas and Nephele; stepson of Ino; flees from stepmother's schemes with his sister, Helle, on a golden ram; arriving in Colchis, he sacrifices the ram and gives its golden fleece to King Aeetes, the father of Medea*

Medea: *the daughter of King Aeetes; she is acquainted with magic and uses it on behalf of Jason, who seduces her*

Hecate: *goddess of enchantment and the world of night; she predates the Olympians*

Aeson: *deposed king of Thessaly; father of Jason*

Glaucus: *a fisherman who eats a magic herb and becomes a sea god pursues the nymph Scylla, who becomes a rock*

Pelias: *half-brother of Aeson; usurper of this throne*

Cerambus: *escapes the flood by being turned into a beetle*

Aegeus: *king of Athens; father of Theseus*

Theseus: *celebrated hero of Athens; son of Aegeus*

Minos: *king of Crete; son of Jove and Europa*

Androgeos: *son of Minos; treacherously slain in Athens during a contest*

Summary

The Argonauts went sailing for the Golden Fleece, rescued Phineus from the Harpies, and arrived in Colchis, where they asked for the return of the fleece. The king made outrageous demands as prerequisites, but his daughter, Medea, fell passionately in love with the leader of the expedition and, after an intense inner struggle, decided to help him. She went to Hecate's old altar and met Jason face to face. He promised to marry her if she would help him. She provided him with magic herbs and good advice, and he fulfilled the king's demands. Medea even helped him steal the fleece from its secret hiding place and the dragon set to guard it.

Jason took Medea home with him, where she proved her magic powers again by restoring Aeson, the exiled king, to youthful vigor. Finally, she arranged a clever way to dispatch the usurper, King Pelias. But when she returned from this last mission, a shock awaited her: Jason had taken a new bride. Medea killed the bride and then, to punish Jason, she killed her own children and escaped "on dragon wings," to Athens.

King Aegeus took her in and married her. Her position was threatened, however, when the king's son, Theseus, arrived in Athens. He had been raised in another country, and his father did not know him. Medea, through her powers as a sorceress, recognized him and tried to kill him with a poisoned drink, but in the last moment, his father recognized Theseus, knocked the poison cup from his hands, and Medea had to flee again.

The people of Athens enjoyed their glory days during the reign of Theseus. But when the son of King Minos was treacherously slain during a visit to Athens, Minos declared war on Athens. He collected many allies, but Aeacus refused to join him; instead, he gave his support to Theseus. While the armies were gathering, Aeacus related how a terrible drought had destroyed his land and people (the work of Juno, who once more exacted vengeance on the whole nation descended from one of Jove's loves, Aegina). When all seemed lost, Jove raised a new people for Aeacus, the Myrmidons, seemingly transformed from a swarm of ants.

Cephalus, one of the princes of Athens, told his tragic story. He and his wife Procris were happily married. This time, it was a goddess who was to blame for the end of their bliss. She fell in love with Cephalus and tried to seduce him. When he refused, she planted a doubt in his mind about his wife's faithfulness to him. Foolishly, he "put her to the test" and almost destroyed their love. After his wife forgave him, she presented him with a wonderful hunting dog. But this time it was his wife who had been persuaded that he was unfaithful to her. Trying to get proof one way or another, while he was out hunting, she came too close to him, eavesdropping, and he mistook her for an animal, killing her with his spear.

Analysis

The story of the Golden Fleece and the Argonauts was so well known to Ovid's readers that he took it for granted that they understood the many allusions contained in this part of the poem. Some of the major facts of the story are omitted altogether; instead, Ovid concentrates on the mental states of Medea and some of the more wondrous incidents in the story. In these, he was aided by the extensive training he had received as a youth in the art of rhetoric. He had also written a play, *Medea*, which was much admired, but which is unfortunately lost; this incident is full of drama. The story of Medea and Jason is one of the most brilliant parts of the *Metamorphoses*, and one into which Ovid put his greatest gifts of psychological insight and poetic skill.

To understand this part of the poem, some background is necessary.

The Greeks, a seafaring people, had unbounded admiration for the voyagers of the Argo, a generation before the Trojan War. The journey of the Argonauts, as they were called, was the first major excursion outside of the Mediterranean, into the fabled and fearful area of the Black Sea and the Caucasus.

The villains who set things into motion were two people Ovid had depicted as hapless victims of Juno's ire earlier in the poem: Athamas and Ino. Athamas, King of Thebes, had set his first wife, Nephele, aside, and married Ino. Nephele was fearful for the fate of her own children, and a golden ram was sent to rescue the boy, Phrixus, and the girl, Helle. As they were escaping across the strait which separates Europe from Asia, Helle slipped from the ram's back and drowned; the Hellespont is named after her. Phrixus arrived in Colchis and, inexplicably, sacrificed the ram which had saved him, presenting its fleece to the King of Colchis, Aeetes.

A generation fled by, and a young relative of Phrixus, Jason, heir presumptive to the throne of Thessaly, went to claim the throne of his father Aeson from a usurper, Pelias. Pelias pretended to accede to his wishes but claimed that the spirit of Phrixus demanded that the Golden Fleece be reclaimed from its far-away repository. Jason, brave and adventurous, accepted the challenge, gathered the flower of Greek youth around himself, and set sail for the unknown. Theirs was the greatest story before that of the Trojan War. After innumerable and frightening adventures, they arrived in Colchis. This king, too, pretended to accede to his request, but he also set two impossible tasks to the Argonauts, specifically to Jason, their leader. He had to overcome two wild bulls, yoke them, plow a field with them, and plant the field with dragons' teeth.

The cause of the Argonauts would have been lost right then and there, except for an unexpected turn of events. Medea, the king's daughter, fell passionately in love with Jason. In a long soliloquy, Ovid lets the reader gain a profound insight into a heart of a young woman who has to set aside her loyalty to her father— accepted unquestioningly up to that time—in favor of a stranger who fills her with an uncontrollable desire. She gives him all the help he needs: magic herbs and strategic advice. But the king plots treason; he plans to kill Jason. Medea informs Jason of the plan; she begs him to take her with him. In exchange she helps him to obtain the fleece by putting the guardian dragon to sleep. In a fuller version of the story, which Ovid omitted, Medea even sacrificed her own brother's life to get Jason's promise to wed her. In tracing the changes in the feelings and modes of behavior in Medea, Ovid introduced a new kind of metamorphosis: an inexperienced girl becomes a mature, passionate woman. Her tragedy is that she has fixed her passion on the wrong man.

Returning to Greece with Jason, Medea rejuvenates the deposed old king, Aeson; she even undertakes the treacherous murder of the usurper, Pelias. But Jason proves unworthy of her love; in her absence, he prepares to marry another woman. When Medea finds out his betrayal, she kills the new bride with a poisonous garment, and then, to inflict the greatest possible suffering on Jason, she murders her own children. Luckily for her, she is the granddaughter of the Sun and is able to escape in a chariot provided by him.

Her next adventure lands her in Athens, where the king, Aegeus, falls in love with her and marries her. The arrival of the king's son, Theseus, threatens her position. After an unsuccessful attempt to kill Theseus, she has to flee again, proving once more that divine descent can provide some guarantees not available to ordinary mortals.

The rest of the book deals briefly with some of the great deeds of Theseus. These, too, were so well known that Ovid sums them up in a few lines. Then he concentrates on the preparations for the war between Athens and Crete, giving himself occasion to relate two tales: the origin of the Myrmidons, and the story of Cephalus and Procris.

Study Questions

1. What are the contradictory claims in Medea's heart while she soliloquizes?

2. The story of the dragons' teeth echoes what earlier episode?

3. How did Jason overcome the "sown men"?

4. What well-known incident did Ovid omit after Jason's victory over the bulls?

5. Ovid gives Jason an altruistic aspect with respect to his father. What is it?

6. What is the magic number connected with the cult of Hecate?

7. What was the most monstrous aspect of Medea's treatment of Pelias?

8. What device does Ovid employ to sum up the deeds of Theseus?

9. Why did Juno hate Aeacus and his country?

10. In what important aspect is the story of Cephalus and Procris different from other accounts of relationships between males and females?

Answers

1. Medea feels that she ought to be loyal to her father, yet she loves a stranger. Her sexual passion makes her disregard the social norms of her time.

2. The story of Cadmus also included the motif of "sown men."

3. Jason, following Medea's advice, threw a stone among the "sown men."

4. Ovid fails to mention Medea's treacherous murder of her brother to aid Jason. This is the first incident in an escalating series of desperate measures in which Medea violates the Golden Mean in attempting to secure her own power vis-a-vis a man.

5. Jason offers to give up some years of his own life to add them to his father's life.

6. Hecate, the "triple-goddess" has the number three connected with her cult.

7. Medea induced the daughters of Pelias to cut up their own father.

8. The deeds of Theseus are summed up in a hymn of praise to him.

9. Juno hated Aeacus and his country because the king's mother, Aegina, was one of the nymphs Jove had seduced.

10. The story of Cephalus and Procris shows a genuinely loving relationship between a male and female. Significantly, these two are mortals, not gods.

Suggested Essay Topics

1. In this book, Ovid makes the most important change in his poem so far. He shifts from the relationships of gods and mortals to relationships among mortals. Give examples and comments on the effect of this change on you, the reader.

2. In Medea's great soliloquy, Ovid made use of many of the rhetorical devices taught to him in the course of his excellent education, intended to make him a candidate for political

office. Analyze Medea's soliloquy as a model speech, such as one would use for persuasion.

Book VIII

New Characters:

Nisus: *king of Megara; father of Nisus*

Scylla: *daughter of Nisus; betrays her father to ingratiate herself with King Minos; changed into a bird*

Daedalus: *Athenian inventor and architect; father of Icarus; dreams of flight lead to tragedy*

Icarus: *son of Daedalus; participates in father's dreams of flight with tragic results*

Ariadne: *a princess of Crete*

Minotaur: *a monster, half-man and half-bull, who resides on Crete*

Meleager: *son of Oeneus, king of Calydon, and Althaea; becomes an Argonaut*

Castor and Pollux: *twin brothers who become constellations; sons of Leda, who was raped by Jove*

Atalanta: *a young woman from Arcadia, she is a champion hunter and a warrior*

Plexippus and Toxeus: *uncles of Meleager*

Althaea: *mother of Meleager; sister of Plexippus and Toxeus*

Deianira and Gorge: *sisters of Meleager*

Oeneus: *putative father of Meleager*

Achelous: *a river god*

Pirithous and Lelex: *hunters who are Meleager's fellow woodsmen*

Philomen and Baucis: *a pious old couple*

Erysichthon: *a king who offends Ceres*

Mestra: *daughter of Erysichthon; she is not named in the story, but Ovid's contemporaries knew who she waas*

Summary

While Cephalus was returning home with his new army, Minos was laying siege to Megara, where King Nisus reigned. During the siege, the king's daughter, Scylla, spent her time watching the soldiers below. From her vantage point, she came to know King Minos of Crete, and fell in love with him. She convinced herself that if she stole down to the enemy and offered herself as a hostage, the hostilities would cease; more important to her, Minos would return her love. She executed her plan, but the righteous Minos repulsed her in horror; she ended up as a wretched sea-bird.

Minos, however, had troubles at home. His wife had conceived a monstrous passion for a bull, lured it to herself while disguised as a cow, and had an offspring by the bull, the Minotaur, half-man, half-bull. To hide the family shame, Minos engaged Daedalus, a master builder, to construct a maze, a labyrinth, to contain the Minotaur. Every nine years, seven youths and seven maidens had to be sacrificed to it. These were chosen from among the young people of Athens, which Minos had defeated. On the third occasion, Theseus volunteered to be included among the intended members of the tribute. With the help of Ariadne, the daughter of Minos, he was able to penetrate the labyrinth, slay the monster, and get out again. Ariadne eloped with him, but he abandoned her on the island of Dia, at Naxos. She was rescued by Bacchus who set her chaplet into the heavens as a constellation.

Daedalus, held prisoner by Minos so he could not reveal the secret of the Labyrinth, became so homesick that he devised a means to escape by air. He fashioned wings for himself and his son Icarus from feathers and wax. Icarus could not contain his enthusiasm, flew too close to the sun, and—since the wax holding the feathers together melted—fell into the sea and drowned.

Daedalus could be cruel, too. He became jealous of the inventions of his young nephew, Perdix, and pushed him from the Acropolis of Athens. The boy was saved by becoming a bird, a partridge, but ever after was afraid of heights.

Theseus was so renowned for his great deeds that a prince of Calydon, Meleager, called on him for help in his time of trouble. King Oeneus, grateful for a good harvest, had honored all the gods but omitted Diana. Offended, she sent a curse on his land, a gigantic boar which laid the land to waste. Meleager invited all the famous heroes of Greece to help conquer the boar. They came eagerly, among them such notables as Peleus, later father of Achilles, and Laertes, father of Ulysses. Also present was "The pride of Arcadian woodlands, Atalanta." Meleager was very much attracted to her, but he put business first: the hunt. At first, the boar seemed invulnerable, but Atalanta's arrow found its mark and bloodied the beast. In the end, it was Meleager who slew the boar, but, in tribute to her marksmanship and also of his admiration for her, he awarded the trophy to Atalanta. His boorish uncles took violent exception to his judgment in making a girl the victor of the hunt; they took the trophy from her and also insulted him. In a rage, he stabbed them to death.

Meleager's mother, Althaea, was celebrating her son's success when she learned of the death of her brothers; her shock was magnified when she found out that it was her own son who had killed them. She was presented with a tremendous dilemma. Family loyalty demanded that she avenge the murder of her blood kin, her brothers, but she also loved her son deeply. She alone knew that she had it in her power to end his life due to a special log, a brand, presented to her by the Fates at the time of her son's birth. As long as this log existed, Meleager was immortal. After much soul-searching, she destroyed the log. Meleager, unaware of all this, went into a swift decline and died. Althaea killed herself. His sisters, in their grief, were turned into birds by Diana, except for two, Gorge and Deianira.

Theseus, the hunt over, was on his way home when his passage was blocked by a swollen river. The river-god, Achelous, invited him and his companions to wait in his palatial cave for the flooding to subside. They whiled away the time of waiting with stories. Achelous himself told of some of his past affairs with naiads and also with an unfortunate girl, Perimele. All of these were turned into islands. Pirithous doubted that there was such a thing as a metamorphosis, but Lelex, another of the travelers, introduced the story of Philemon and Baucis, the pious and hospitable couple, who entertained Jove and Mercury and, as a reward, were permitted to turn into loving trees, side by side. Lelex announced the moral: "The gods look after / Good people still, and cherishers are cherished."

Prompted by Theseus, the host told another story, reminding the audience of Proteus, who could change his form at will, and also that of the daughter of Erysichthon. Erysichthon scorned the gods; he even cut down the sacred oak of Ceres. The goddess punished him with insatiable hunger. His daughter tried to provide for him, but in the end he even sold her for money. The girl cried to Neptune, who changed her into a fisherman so she could elude her master. For a while, the father capitalized on the daughter's talent to change her shape, but in the end he even consumed his own flesh.

Achelous concluded by mentioning that he himself had been able to change into different forms and pointed to the fact that he had only one horn on his forehead, the other was gone. Then he groaned.

Analysis

The series of traitorous women—such as Medea—who had betrayed father and country, continues in this Book. Only one, Arne, did it for gold; she is dismissed with a brief mention in the catalog of the allies of Minos. Scylla did it for love and was scorned by Minos. Ariadne was abandoned by Theseus after helping him overcome the Minotaur.

The figure of Minos is surrounded by bull-imagery. His father, Jove, had seduced Europa in the guise of a bull. His wife, Pasiphaë, likewise, became enamored of a bull and conceived a monster. In modern times, when archeologists excavated Crete and its capital, Knossos, they were struck by the images of giant horns shaped like crescent moons. On the walls of its maze-like capital, vivid scenes depicted rituals involving boys and girls leaping, acrobat-like, over the horns of charging bulls. Something of this bull-cult must have been noticed by the conquering Achaians, an early Greek tribe which rose to dominance at that time. They marveled at the ruins of Crete, a civilization much more ancient and advanced than their own. In the Cretan myths, Zeus (later called Jove by the Romans) was born on their island. The Greeks were not prepared to accept that. At most, they conceded he may have been raised there. By the time of the Trojan War, Crete had been laid low several times by earthquake and fire and had become an ally of the Achaian chiefs under Agamemnon and Menelaus.

It is believed that the Cretans had worshipped the Great Mother as the ruler of life and death, with her symbol of the sacred labrum, an axe shaped like two crescent moons, or bull-horns placed back-to-back. Her astoundingly modern royal palace was like a maze, with many rooms, and built on different levels; from its name, "The House of the Labrum," was derived the word *labyrinth*. Minos was in all likelihood not a single individual's name but a dynastic title, like pharaoh. But an archetypal image of Minos, a great and just king prevailed; Greek and Roman myth made him one of the judges of the Underworld.

The name of Daedalus, too, became a household word, signifying a type of resourceful man, a practical genius. The incident of his son's fall into the Icarian sea is the subject of a famous painting by the artist Brueghel. Together with Phaëthon, the boy became a symbol of the recklessness of some youths. It is remarkable that immediately after showing us Daedalus, the grieving father, Ovid employs a sophisticated form of irony: the poetic device of the "divided attitude of the author toward his own creation." The grieving father now becomes the cruel uncle, ruthlessly destroying the gifted boy who could become his rival in fame.

The following episodes are linked by the presence of Theseus, either as participant or listener. At no point is he allowed to occupy center stage.

As the fame of Theseus grew abroad, he was invited to the Calydonian boar-hunt. This story was based on a lost drama of Euripides and was a great favorite in antiquity, both in literature and the arts. A miniature epic, it follows many of the epic traditions, including the catalog of heroes and battlefield scenes reduced to scenes of the chase. The extreme size of the boar makes the whole story grotesque, almost a *pastiche* of an epic poem; the heroes are not of the magnitude of true epic heroes, conducting themselves fairly ineffectively. It is to be observed that some of them are the fathers of the heroes of the Trojan War. The true interest lies in the relationship between Meleander and Atalanta. He, for once, is a true gentleman; she a noble forerunner of the Amazon queen Penthesilea whom Achilles defeats in single combat.

In the tragic aftermath, Meleager's mother delivers the same kind of rhetorical soliloquy as Medea did in the preceding book. The modern reader is at a loss to understand how Althaea's loyalty to her brothers (who represent the worst kind of sexism, even for their time) could outweigh her duty toward, and love for, her son. The motif of the brand on which someone's life depended may go back to an ancient folk-tale. The exaggerated grief of the sisters of Meleander maybe traced to another ancient source which introduces Deianira, future wife of Hercules.

Theseus then reappears to provide a somewhat clumsy transition to the next episodes. Achelous, both god and river, provides temporary shelter to the hunters returning home; the conversation turns to the subject of "changing one's shape." The most famous of the stories is that of Philemon and Baucis, a favorite of ancient authors. It is one of the few episodes in the *Metamorphoses* featuring a happily married couple, albeit an old one. Their home and mode of living is a throw-back to the Golden Age of myth. The joint appearance of Jove and Mercury in the tale suggests a cult of them in this region; it even has an echo in the Christian New Testament, when the slightly built but eloquent Apostle Paul was mistaken for Mercury, and his impressive-looking disciple Barnabas for Jove. (Acts 14: 11-12.) The episode concludes with a charming testimony of ancient tree-worship.

The story of the saintly old couple is contrasted by its opposite: Erysichthon is guilty of a sacrilege involving a tree. His punishment for cutting down the sacred oak of Ceres is severe indeed, bringing misfortune not only on him but on his whole country. Only the figure of his obliging daughter relieves the dark picture, introducing a momentary comic relief. Achelous provides the transition to the next book by suggesting that he himself had at one time been able to change his shape repeatedly.

Study Questions

1. What was the guarantee of Nisus' being able to keep his kingdom?

2. Ovid dismisses the outcome of the war in half a line. What was it?

3. What was the punishment of Scylla?

4. How did Minos show his gratitude to Jove?

5. What was the double relationship of Minos to bulls in the myths?

6. How does Ovid suggest in advance that Icarus will die?

7. How is the behavior of Meleander different from that of most other men with respect to women?

8. What was the dilemma of Althaea?

9. Wherein lies the injustice in the fate of Perimele?

10. What role does Pirithous perform during the tales of transformations?

Answers

1. Nisus had a single purple lock; his ability to retain the kingdom depended on it.

2. Ovid says of Minos simply, "his enemies were conquered."

3. Scylla was changed to a bird, pursued by another bird, formerly her father.

4. He sacrificed a hundred bulls, as he had vowed to do.

5. Minos' mother, Europa, was abducted by Jove in the guise of a bull; his wife Pasiphaë became enamored of a bull and had offspring by him: the Minotaur.

6. Daedalus kissed his son. (Goodbye, if he had known it.)

7. He treats Atalanta with respect even though he is attracted to her. He acknowledges her role in the success of the hunt and awards the trophy to her. When criticized for this, he defends his actions.

8. Althaea feels she has to avenge the murder of her brothers, even at the price of killing her own son, whom she loves dearly.

9. Perimele was ravished by Achelous and was murdered by her own father for "unchastity."

10. Pirithous plays "devil's advocate." By expressing doubts about the possibility of someone changing shapes, he induces first Lelex, then Achelous to tell more such tales.

Suggested Essay Topics

1. What do Medea, Scylla, and Ariadne have in common? What was their motivation, what act did they perform, and what was their "reward"? In sum, what was antiquity's (and Ovid's) judgment concerning women who do what they did?

2. The stories of Philemon and Baucis on the one hand, and Erysichthon on the other share the common motif of respect for trees. Is there a lesson in them for our own times? Explain.

Book IX

New Characters:

Hercules: *a celebrated hero. known for his strength; son of Jove with Alcmena*

Nessus: *a centaur in love with Deinaira*

Iole: *a princess captured by Hercules*

Lichas: *a servant of Deinaira*

Geryon, Cerberus, Hydra, etc.: *victims of Hercules during his Twelve Labors*

Philoctetes: *son of Poeas; friend of Hercules*

Eurystheus: *king of Mycenae; at Juno's command, imposes the Twelve Labors on Hercules*

Hyllus: *son of Hercules*

Ilithyia (Lucina): *goddess of childbirth*

Galanthis: *servant girl of Alcmena*

Dryope: *half-sister of Alcmena; mother of Amphissus with Apollo; married by Andraemon*

Lotis: *a naiad, pursued by Priapus, the god of gardens and vineyards*

Iolaus: *nephew and companion of Hercules; when Hercules asks Hebe, Iolaus is rejuvenated*

Hebe: *daughter of Juno; given to Hercules as a wife after he is made a god*

Capaneus: *Argive chief; one of the Seven Against Thebes*

Callirhoe: *gains special grace from Jove*

Iasion: *beloved by Ceres*

Anchises: *mortal father of Aeneas*

Aeacus: *son of Jove by Aegina*

Radamanthus: *one of the judges of the underworld, with Minos and Aeacus; a son of Jove*

Miletus: *a son of Apollo and Deione*

Maeander: *a river turning on itself*

Cyane: *a nymph changed by Pluto into a pool*

Caunus and Byblis: *children of Cyane and Miletus*

Ops: *ancient deity; wife of Saturn in Roman beliefs*

Thetys: *wife of Ocean in the pre-Olympian times; not to be confused with Thetis, a sea nymph who is the wife of Peleus and the mother of Achilles*

Sons of Aeolus: *certain of these men committed incest with their sisters*

Ligdus and Telethusa: *parents of Iphis*

Inachus: *father of Io; after she flees to Egypt, she becomes a manifestation of the goddess Isis*

Anubis, Bubastis Apis, Harpocrates, Osiris: *ancient Egyptian divinities whose history had reached the Roman empire when Ovid was writing*

Ianthe: *daughter of Teleses, chosen by Ligdus as a wife for Iphis*

Hymen: *the god of marriage*

Summary

Achelous became a rival of Hercules for the hand of Deianeira. Although he was able to transform himself first into a serpent and then a bull, Hercules just laughed at him; for him, this was child's play. Achelous lost one of his bull's horns during their wrestling match. Hercules had another disgruntled rival, the centaur Nessus; he tried to rape Deianeira and was shot by Hercules. As his revenge, he gave a magic robe to Deianeira, pretending that it would keep her husband faithful. When rumors of Hercules' relationship with Iole reached her, the worried wife sent him the robe; this set his whole body on fire. To escape the unbearable pain, the hero built a funeral pyre for himself and had his friend Philoctetes light it. Jove, the hero's father, rejoiced, for this gave him an opportunity to make his son a god. Even Juno had to accede to the divine decree.

Hercules' wish was that Iole should marry his son Hyllus. His mother, Alcmena, told Iole the story of the birth of Hercules.

Because of her implacable hatred of every woman ever seduced by Jove, Juno tried to prevent the birth of Hercules, but a serving girl loyal to Alcmena lied that the birth had already taken place. Juno turned the girl into a weasel. Alcmena sighed remembering the unjust punishment of her loyal servant. Iole then told her mother-in-law the tragic story of her own sister, Dryope, who was no less innocent of any wrongdoing. Carrying her infant son, she accidentally trespassed on a site which carried a curse. A naiad, Lotis, had been pursued by the god Priapus and escaped only by being turned into a tree. Her prayers unavailing, Dryope, too, was turned into a tree. In a tearful speech, she said goodbye to her little son, husband, and sister Iole.

As Alcmena and Iole were wiping away their tears, they were distracted by a new development. Iolaus, nephew and companion of Hercules, stood before them, rejuvenated. This was the work of Hebe, daughter of Juno. A major argument developed among the Olympian gods whether they, too, could restore their favorite mortals to youth. Jove made two special exemptions but forbade the rest, declaring that only the Fates can determine how long a mortal may live. He pointed to the fact that even he cannot make exceptions after these singular cases. He cited the case of Minos, once so mighty but now old, weak, and consequently threatened by a certain Miletus. Luckily, Miletus gave up the attempted coup, fled to Asia, founded a city, married, and had two children, Caunus and Byblis.

Byblis developed a passion for her own brother. She tried to justify it by reciting to herself all those gods who had married their own sisters, but she knew that "the gods are a law unto themselves," and she, a mere mortal, must not even entertain such thoughts. But in the end she confessed her feelings to her brother, who left the country in horror. Byblis lost her reason and wandered all over the world. In the end, some compassionate naiads sheltered her; Byblis became a fountain.

Another change which occupied people's minds at the time concerned a girl named Iphis. Her father ordered that if the child to be born to his wife should be a girl, she would have to be killed. The mother could not do this; instead, she pretended that the baby was a boy. Fortunately, the name Iphis could belong to either sex. All went well until the father chose a bride for her. In their despair, mother and daughter prayed to Isis—who had suggested the original ruse—and "the next morning made the whole world brighter," Iphis had a sex change and the marriage could take place.

Analysis

With the comic interlude of Achelous' rivalry with Hercules, a cycle of tales begins concerning that hero. Having defeated all other suitors for the hand of Deianira, Hercules had to dispatch the centaur, Nessus, who made an obscene attack on her. Typical of the proprietary attitudes of some males, then and later, he considered his wife his "chattel," shouting, "Let things of mine alone!" Ovid implies that the rumors concerning Hercules and Iole were without foundation, but other ancient sources are not so sure, and his wife was probably justified in trying to ensure his faithfulness. (The revenge of the centaur by means of a poisonous robe reflects an old folk belief.) In any event, it is ironic that this man, or demigod, who had seemed invincible in the face of overwhelming odds, was defeated by love and a person who loved him. But then he who had won his wife with great effort and later neglected her was "rewarded" in Heaven by being given a new, divine bride. So inscrutable were the ways of the Olympians!

The story of the hero's death is now followed by the story of his birth, as told by his mother, Alcmena. Iole, the person of whom Deianira was jealous, actually became the wife of Hercules' son, and Alcmena relates to her the story of the birth of Hercules. Juno wanted to punish her philandering husband through his son and arranged things so that Hercules would be born later than a cousin. The hero had to serve his weakling relative throughout most of his life. In his death-throes he recalled bitterly these enemies of his. He even punished the innocent messenger who had brought him the poisoned robe.

Iole's tale of the metamorphosis of her sister, and that of the naiad Lotis, is one of the most poignant ones in the poem and verbalizes one of the basic tenets of the whole work, that all nature is one, and the spirits of ponds and even of flowers ought to be respected. This profound and noble idea is then followed by a preposterous one, that of the capricious manner in which the lengths of mortal lives are decided. The notion that it is not the gods but the unfathomable Fates who rule the universe was expressed by Homer in one of the most crucial scenes of the *Iliad*, when Zeus (Jove) weighed the fates of the chief adversaries in golden scales. The decision was rendered by some primordial divinities, simply known as The Fates, and all the gods had to abide by their decision. In Ovid's poem, Jove can tinker a little with the Fates' power.

In one of his most contrived transitions, Ovid now turns away from the Hercules-cycle and takes up one of his most controversial cycles of tales, those of what was considered "unnatural love."

To avert criticism, he begins with, for him, an uncharacteristic warning: "Byblis is a warning / That girls should never love what is forbidden. / She loved her brother...." This is a clever way to pretend that he is telling it as a moral lesson instead of a titillating story, and by doing this, he also manages to arouse the interest which adheres to the forbidden.

The love Byblis felt for her brother "Was not the way sisters should love their brothers." She was keenly aware of the "should not" but could not help herself. Her soliloquies, or interior monologues, are masterful arguments, destined to convince herself that she has divine precedent on her side. At the same time, she realizes that divine license does not apply to mortals. She is the master of the paradox: referring to her brother, she says, "All we have / By common bond is a common barrier." Resolving to inform her brother of her feelings by letter, she is repulsed by him and goes insane.

Ovid, ever a master of the dramatic contrast, now introduces an example of an "unnatural love" which did have a happy ending—thanks to a divine intervention. Iphis, victim of her father's sexism, was raised as a male. When he arranged a betrothal for her, she became strongly attracted to her "fiancée; the scandal of a homosexual marriage was avoided by a miracle. Isis, the Egyptian manifestation of the unfortunate Io, changed her into a man. After Julius Caesar conquered Egypt (shortly before the birth of Ovid), the cults of Egyptian divinities became widespread in Rome, and Ovid made clever use of the latest theological fashions.

Study Questions

1. How would you characterize the tone of Ovid in the tale of Achelous' wrestling match with Hercules?

2. Why did Hercules laugh when Achelous changed into a serpent and a bull?

3. What Christian scriptural passage is sometimes believed to be echoed by Hercules' despairing comment, "And men can still believe / In gods!" Why does he say this?

4. How does Jove at last try to make up to his son for all the sufferings he had to endure? What is Juno's reaction?

5. How did Juno try to prevent the birth of Hercules? How was she circumvented?

6. Which earlier tales are recalled by the metamorphoses of Lotis and Dryope?

7. Dryope wants her son to learn a lesson from her tragedy. What is it?

8. In the *Iliad*, the chief god wanted to save his favorite son from death, and his wife rebuked him, saying that if *he* did it, all other gods would want to save *their* favorites. Ovid echoes this idea in the *Metamorphoses*. Identify the passage in which he does this.

9. In an earlier work, Ovid suggested to people in love to make the first declaration in letter form. Here he contradicts that advice. Identify the scene.

10. Iphis almost became a victim of a cruel sexist custom in ancient Greece which is still practiced in some parts of the world. What is it?

Answers

1. Ovid makes the wrestling match scene hilarious.

2. Hercules strangled two serpents, sent by Juno, when he was a baby; he also captured alive a mythical bull in Crete.

3. The sufferings of Hercules and his despairing cry have sometimes been compared to the Passion of Christ and his cry, "My God, my God, why have you forsaken me?" He believes himself forgotten by the gods.

4. Jove compensates Hercules by metamorphosing him into a god. Juno has to demur.

5. As goddess of childbirth, Juno delayed the birth of Hercules, but a servant girl tricked her.

6. Daphne was turned into a laurel, Syrinx into a field of reeds.

7. Dryope wanted her young son to learn "that all the bushes are / Bodies of goddesses."

8. In this poem, several gods and goddesses want to have their favorites rejuvenated, but Jove puts a stop to this.

9. Byblis declares her love to Caunus in a letter but later thinks that this may have been a mistake.

10. Female infanticide—a primitive form of population control —was more widespread in Greece than in Rome but is still practiced in some parts of the world where it is believed that boys are inherently more valuable than girls.

Suggested Essay Topics

1. This book provides ample illustrations of the principle that what is permitted for the gods is not permitted for morals. Give examples.

2. Trace the tortured arguments in the interior monologue of Byblis by reducing it to an outline. This was the kind of rhetorical "homework" favored by the schools attended by students in antiquity; even St. Augustine complained, centuries later, than he had to practice putting himself into the mental states of ancient heroines.

Book X

New Characters:

Orpheus: *a great musician; son of the muse Calliope*

Ixion, Tityos, and the Daughters of Belus: *sufferers in the underworld—the world of the dead*

Eurydice: *wife of Orpheus*

Pluto (Hades): *god of the world of the dead, called the underworld or Dis*

Charon: *boatmen whose cargo is the souls of the dead*

Attis: *a beautiful shepherd beloved by the goddess Cybele*

Cyparissus: *a handsome young man believed to have been invented by Ovid*

Ganymede: *a beautiful boy abducted by Jove to be a cupbearer*

Hyacinthus: *believed of Apollo; probably pre-dates the Olympic pantheon*

Propoetides: *formerly sacred women of Cyprus*

Pygmalion: *a Cyparian who made a statue of a oung woman and fell in love with it*

Galatea: *the transformation name given to the statue*

Paphos: *the daughter of Pygmalion and Galatea*

Cinyras: *the son of Paphos*

Myrrha: *the daughter of Cinyras*

Cencheris: *the wife of Cinyras*

Adonis: *beloved by Venus; son of Myrrha and her father, Cinyras*

Hippomenes: *in love with the swift young woman Atalanta*

Summary

The previous book had a happy end; Book Ten is full of tales of woe. It starts with Orpheus, the magical musician who could charm animals, trees, birds, even the gods, with his singing and his lyre. He loved his bride, Eurydice, but on their wedding day the bride

was bitten by a serpent and died. Orpheus descended to Dis and was so persuasive that the king, Hades, and his queen, Persephone (or Proserpina) gave him the unique opportunity of being allowed to bring his wife back to earth. Unfortunately, he could not abide by the one condition set. On the way up, he turned, in love, to be sure that she was following; in that instant, she was gone. Any further attempts to get her back were useless. Deeply despondent, he left his country.

A handsome youth, called Cyparissus, loved a beautiful deer but accidentally killed it. He grieved so much that Apollo turned him into a cypress. He was one of the many trees which gathered to hear the music of Orpheus. But Apollo himself was unlucky as well: a young man he loved was accidentally killed by a discus thrown by the god. He was turned into a beautiful flower, the hyacinth.

Venus, on the other hand, made some ugly changes. She metamorphosed some unattractive girls first into bulls, then into prostitutes and, eventually, to stone. But she had her merciful side also. Pygmalion, a ruler who was also an accomplished sculptor, disliked the ugly women of the area and decided never to marry. He made a wonderful ivory woman, full-size, and fell in love with her. Since he was a devotee of Venus, the goddess granted his wish and made the statue come to life. They had a daughter, Paphos.

That family, however, was not blessed. Paphos' son, Cinyras, had a daughter, Myrrha, who conceived an unquenchable desire for her own father. She tried to resist but was so unhappy that her nurse pried her secret out of her and arranged things so that Myrrha's wishes were fulfilled without Cinyras' realizing who his lover was. Eventually, though, he discovered her identity and cast her away in horror. Myrrha fled, bore a child, Adonis, and was herself turned into a tree (Myrrh).

Adonis grew up and was so handsome that Venus herself fell passionately in love with him. She became his companion, following him everywhere and teaching him about the secrets of the hunt. During one of their times together, she told him the story of Atalanta.

The girl had heard a prophecy that marriage would cause her to lose her life, and so she decided not to marry. Her many suitors had to compete with her in a foot-race, and the losers had to die. Even so, she had many suitors. One of them, Hippomenes, was aided by Venus. She gave him three golden apples. As they were running, Hippomenes dropped each apple in such a way that Atalanta risked falling behind in order to pick up the apples. She really did not want to win against Hippomenes. They were married, but Hippomenes committed the fatal mistake of not thanking Venus. Her revenge was to lure them into a cave sacred to Cybele; the angry goddess turned them into lions. Venus warns Adonis never to hunt such beasts, "or else your daring / Will be the ruin of us both."

Adonis did not heed the warning, wounded a wild boar, and the enraged animal gored him. All Venus could do for him was to change him into a lovely flower, the anemone.

Analysis

This is perhaps the darkest book of the *Metamorphoses:* whatever happiness comes to the characters disappears almost immediately. Orpheus is married; his bride dies on their wedding day. He reclaims her, only to lose her again. The stories he tells are all unhappy also, their subjects being "unnatural loves." The final few lines sum it all up best: the flowers "as briefly clinging / To life as did Adonis....Doomed all to swift and soon."

The myth of Orpheus and Eurydice is among the most famous of ancient myths still. At least three operas were inspired by it, works of the composers Monteverdi, Gluck, and Offenbach. Several painters and sculptors have found inspiration in it also.

The tale of Pygmalion and Galatea also became a fountain of inspiration for writers and artists. (A well-known literary adaptation is G. B. Shaw's *Pygmalion*.)

In some versions of the Atalanta myth, the two Atalantas are the same. Whether or not there was a prophecy warning her against marriage, she had ample reasons to want to avoid becoming subjected to men. She was a superb athlete and hunter. Because of her earlier tragic association with Meleager, and the crude and cruel sexist treatment she received at the hands of Meleager's uncles, depriving her of her well-deserved trophy just because she was a woman, she came to hate all men. Wanting to prove that "Anything you can do, I can do better," she instituted the foot-race; this gave her ample opportunities for revenge against men. She

did not mind marrying Hippomenes, once she fell in love with him, even though he had tricked her, but, unfortunately, the prophecy was fulfilled and the marriage did cost her dearly when Venus changed her and her husband into lions.

In telling this tale to Adonis, Venus endorses the idea, expounded at length by Pythagoras in Book Fifteen, of the connectedness of all life.

Study Questions

1. What warning does Ovid give that Orpheus' marriage will be unhappy?

2. How does Orpheus explain his unusual request to the gods of the underworld?

3. What is the reaction of the shades in Hades?

4. What taboo does Orpheus break on their way up?

5. What are the two ways in which Hyacinthus is remembered?

6. Why was Venus angry at the women of Cyprus?

7. What is meant by: "The best art is that which conceals art?"

8. Pygmalion's behavior toward Venus is different from that of Hippomenes. Explain. Venus' attitude toward them is different also. Explain.

9. How does Ovid distance himself from the story of Myrrha and Cinyras?

10. In what new role do we see Venus in the tale of Adonis?

Answers

1. No blessing came on the young couple from Hymen; the torch sputtered.

2. He is only asking a loan of Eurydice, for her unspent years.

3. Everyone is deeply moved; even the Furies weep.

4. Orpheus turns and looks back; this was forbidden.

5. His name survives in a flower; the people hold a festival in his memory.

6. The women were murderers and brought shame to the goddess' birthplace.

7. The ancients believed that when looking at a work of art, one should not be aware that it is art and not the real thing.

8. Hippomenes failed to thank Venus and was punished; Pygmalion thanked her and lived happily with his bride.

9. Ovid takes trouble to warn the reader either not to read this story, or not to believe it, but at least to realize that the "crime" was punished; at any rate, the readers should be happy that those events happened far away.

10. In this episode, Venus, the goddess, behaves like any simple girl in love.

Suggested Essay Topics

1. Several episodes in this book and the preceding one portray "guilt by association," a questionable principle. Discuss the cases in which the capricious divinities inflict punishments on a whole nation because of a transgression of a single individual. How do you feel about this kind of "divine justice?"

2. Discuss the cases in which an individual was punished because of some innocent transgression. Do you feel that a person can be punished for committing an act that was unintentional? What about cases of compulsion which the person could not help?

Book XI

New Characters:

Midas: *king of Phrygia; known for his lack of taste, judgment and wisdom; be careful what you wish for because you might get it*

Silenus: *a satyr; foster father of Bacchus (Dionysus), the god of wine and ecstasty*

Eumolphus: *singer; priest of Ceres*

Pan: *the god of the woods and of shepherds*

Laomedon: *king of Troy; father of Priam*

Hesione: *a Trojan princess*

Thetis: *a sea nymph; mother of Achilles*

Ceyx: *king of Trachis; husband of Alcyone*

Daedalion: *brother of Ceyx; father of Chione*

Chione: *daughter of Daedalion; pursued by Apollo and Mercury; bore Philammon and Autolycus*

Oneton: *a herdsman of Peleus*

Acastus: *king of Magnesia*

Morpheus: *son of Somnus; the god of sleep*

Aesacus: *half brother of Hector*

Hesperie: *a nymph, beloved of Aesacus*

Summary

Trees, beasts, and stones followed the magical song of Orpheus. But the ecstasy-maddened Ciconian women—followers of Bacchus —were angry at him because he had avoided women since the death of his wife. In their drug-induced ritual trance, they tore him to pieces. Apollo stopped their frenzy; in Hades, Orpheus was reunited with the shade of his Eurydice.

But Bacchus disapproved of the excesses of his devotees and turned them into oaks. Then he left the area and went to Mt. Timolus and the river Pactolus. One of his favorite satyrs, Silenus, was missing; perhaps he had too much wine to drink. Midas and

Eumolpus were both devotees of Bacchus; Midas brought Silenus back to Bacchus, who wished to reward him. The god made an unbreakable promise to Midas that he would fulfill any of his wishes. Midas, foolishly, asked that anything he touched might turn to gold. The wish was fulfilled, but Midas soon regretted it, for even food and drink were transformed into gold, and he nearly died of hunger and thirst. Fortunately, Bacchus took back the "reward".

But Midas was still foolish. When Pan challenged Apollo to a music contest, and Apollo won, Midas was dissatisfied and insisted that Pan was the better musician. Apollo, in a pique, gave him asses' ears.

Then Apollo flew to the site where Laomedon was building the walls of his new city, Troy. Apollo, together with the god Neptune, completed the city walls, but Laomedon broke his promise and did not pay them. Neptune was so angry that he flooded the plain on which the city stood; he also demanded that Princess Hesione be sacrificed to him. Although Hercules saved the princess, Laomedon denied the debt a second time; so Hercules gave the princess as a prize to his friend Telamon. Peleus, another ally, was given the goddess Thetis for a bride.

That marriage was the result of a prophecy. Proteus told Thetis that her son would be greater than his father. Jove, not wanting anyone to become greater than himself, resisted the temptation to make love to Thetis and instead gave her to a mortal man, Peleus. Thetis tried to escape, but she was raped by Peleus. Their son became the famous Achaian warrior Achilles.

But Peleus had a great sorrow. He was guilty of the accidental death of his own brother, Phocus. Fleeing, he found a kind reception by King Ceyx of Thracis, who told him the story of Daedalion, his brother, though his opposite in character. Ceyx was kind and peace-loving; Daedalion was aggressive and violent. Daedalion had a daughter, Chione, who was so lovely that two gods made love to her; she bore a son to each. She was so vain of her twins that she offended Diana. The goddess killed her with an arrow. Daedalion, in his grief over the loss of his daughter, jumped off a cliff. Apollo turned him into a hawk.

When Ceyx finished his story, a servant rushed in, with a tale of a ravenous wolf killing the cattle of Peleus. Peleus saw in this a

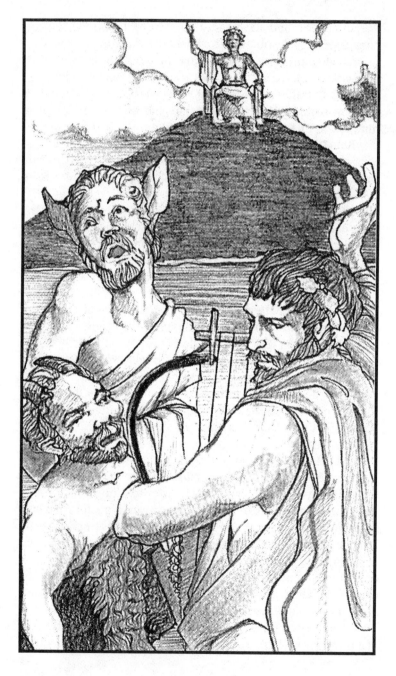

punishment for his secret guilt, fratricide. He prayed for forgiveness. Eventually, he obtained it, in another country.

King Ceyx, who was not aware of his brother Daedalion's fate, then started out to consult an oracle. His loving wife, Alcyone, begged him not to go, but he felt compelled to do so and left by sea. His ship ran into a terrible storm, and he perished. His wife was unaware of it, and offered so many prayers for his homecoming that Juno was disturbed. Technically, Alcyone was a widow and it was wrong for her to offer sacrifices which were proper for a living person but not for someone already dead. So Juno sent a divine messenger, the son of the god Sleep, to show her in a dream that her husband was dead. When Alcyone realized that her husband had drowned, she rushed to the seashore. Miraculously, her husband's corpse was drifting toward the shore just then. She hurled herself into the waves, but instead of drowning, she became a sea-bird, and her husband soon joined her, circling above the waters. During their brooding periods, the sea is calm, and so, from her name, calm periods in life are called "halcyon days." Still another bird-metamorphosis occurred when Aesacus pursued Hesperia so violently that she, in her flight, startled a snake, was bitten by it, and died. In his remorseful grief, Aesacus tried to drown himself but was instead metamorphosed into a bird, one which dives deep into the water.

Analysis

The tragic ending of Orpheus reflects the excesses that the worshippers of Bacchus were capable of. There was an ancient tradition that the head and lyre of the singer were washed up on the island of Lesbos and, ever since, that island has become pre-eminent in song and poetry. It is poetic justice that the Maenads who killed him were turned into trees, symbolically joining the other trees which had been enchanted by the poet's music. The happy ending with Euridyce was Ovid's addition to the tale.

The tale of Midas was also much simpler before Ovid developed it. A folk-tale illustrating the proverb that an unmusical person is like a donkey listening to the lyre became an amusing and well-rounded story in its own right; it then became joined to the teaching story of a greedy man who was punished by having his foolish wish fulfilled. The lesson provided by Midas has become one of the best-known parts of Ovid's great poem.

The story of Ceyx and Alcyone is considered by some critics the most beautiful and moving episode in the entire *Metamorphoses*. It is certainly one of the chief examples of an important subsidiary theme of the poem: the sad inevitability of death and the difficulty some people have in accepting it. Unrestrained sorrow brought on by the death of a loved one often leads to suicide or a change from being a man or woman into something else such as a fountain or a sea-bird. The intervention of the gods to save these unbalanced souls from total annihilation through metamorphoses recognizes the validity of the grief but moralizes that nothing should be carried to extremes (the principle of the Golden Mean).

A cursory reference to a trip taken by Apollo provides the transition to a major new topic: the Trojan War and its antecedents. As Edwin J. Kenney points out in his excellent notes to the Melville translation of this poem, "For the ancients, in so far as a distinction was made between history and myth, the Trojan War tended to mark the dividing line." That war occupies the next three Books of the poem. Here, we are introduced to its antecedents: the building of the walls of Troy, the treachery of King Laomedon, and the story of Peleus and Thetis, the parents of Achilles. Then, after inserting the sad story of Ceyx and Alcyone, Ovid introduces another Trojan personage, Aesacus, leading the reader up to the main narratives of the Trojan War.

Study Questions

1. Why did the Ciconian women kill Orpheus?

2. What happened to his body and his ghost?

3. How did Bacchus respond to the acts of his crazed devotees?

4. Identify Midas, Eumolpus, and Silenus.

5. What was the foolish wish of Midas? What was the result?

6. How did Midas acquire "asses' ears?"

7. What did Princess Hesione and the goddess Thetis have in common?

8. Why was the punishment of Daedalion appropriate to his personality?

9. Why was the punishment of Aesacus appropriate to his behavior?

10. What is the origin of the expression "halcyon days?"

Answers

1. The Ciconian women resented the fact that Orpheus avoided women. Also, they were drunk and drugged.

2. Parts of his body were washed up and were venerated; his ghost went to Dis and was reunited with Eurydice.

3. Bacchus punished his crazed devotees by turning them into trees. He was rather inconsistent; earlier, he had punished Pentheus for *not* participating in his orgies.

4. Eumolpus was a devotee of Ceres; Silenus worshipped Bacchus, his foster-son. Midas found the tipsy old man and restored him to Bacchus.

5. Midas foolishly asked that everything he touched might turn to gold. As a result, he could neither eat nor drink anything.

6. Midas insisted that Pan was a better musician than Apollo; his ears were made into asses' ears as a punishment.

7. Princess Hesione was awarded as a prize; the goddess was given in marriage against her will. Both were treated by males like chattel.

8. The punishment of Daedalion was appropriate because he was an aggressive person and therefore was turned into an aggressive bird.

9. The punishment of Aesacus was appropriate because he repeatedly dove into the sea and therefore was turned into a diving bird.

10. The term "halcyon days" originated in the fact that Alcyone and her husband were turned into birds which brood over quiet waters.

Suggested Essay Topics

1. Many of the metamorphoses in this Book are punishments for individual transgressions. The theme, "to make the punishment fit the crime," is generally quite obvious. But the punishment of Laomedon was quite out of proportion with his transgression: his refusal to pay a debt led to the eventual destruction of his whole city and its people. Comment on "divine justice" in this Book. What about human justice? Does it still happen that one nation "judges" another and then destroys it?

2. The female characters in this Book range all the way from the crazed Ciconians to the saintly Alcyone, and many shadings in-between. Comment on Ovid's skill in introducing so many different female characters. What does this say about stereotypical comments, such as "All women are..."

Book XII

New Characters:

Priam: *the last king of Troy*

Hector: *Priam's most valiant son*

Paris: *another son of Priam; his abduction of Helen leads to the Trojan War*

Calchas: *an interpreter of dreams*

Nereus: *a sea god or the sea itself*

Agamemnon: *king of Mycanae; leader of the Greek forces against Troy*

Iphigenia: *daughter of Agamemnon*

Protesilaus: *first victim of the war*

Cygnus: *one of several heroes with the same name; each is changed into a swan*

Menoetes: *a victim of Achilles*

Nestor: *king of Pylos*

Caeneus: *born a girl, Caenis, and changed into a male; invinvible hero*

Ixion: *king of the Lapithae; ancestor of the centaurs by a cloud*

Pirithous: *son of Ixion with a mortal mother*

Hippodame: *wife of Pirithous*

Eurytus: *a wild centaur*

Many of the Lapithae and centaurs: *killed in the melee caused by Eurytus*

Cyllarus: *a handsome centaur in love with Hylonome*

Tiepolemus: *son of Hercules*

Diomedes: *Greek hero*

Ajax the Lesser: *son of Oileus; Greek hero*

Menelaus: *king of Sparta; husband of Helen; brother of Agamemnon*

Ulysses and Ajax the Greater: *contenders for the armor of Achilles*

Summary

At the tomb Priam erected for his son, Aesacus, not knowing that the son was alive as a bird, all his sons presented sacrifices except Paris. Soon after Aesacus' tragedy, Paris abducted Helen and brought long warfare on his country. The Greeks swore vengeance, a thousand ships were launched, and the only thing that held them back was a lack of favorable winds. At the port of Aulis, the Greek warriors and their leaders were offering a sacrifice for Jove, but a very bad omen warned them that, even though they would eventually destroy Troy, it would take them nine years to do so. Moreover, the goddess Diana was offended and only the blood of a virgin would appease her. Agamemnon, Lord of Hosts, was persuaded that his virgin daughter Iphigenia was to be the victim. The goddess substituted a deer—secretly, so the Greeks did not know it—and finally the ships could sail.

Rumor reached Troy about the onslaught, and Priam's soldiers were ready. Hector, Priam's eldest and bravest son, killed his first Greek, and Cygnus, son of Neptune, "slew his thousands." Achilles swore to kill one of these two; Hector eluded him, and Cygnus proved to be invulnerable to weapons. Achilles finally subdued

Cygnus by pinning him to the ground, stripping off his helmet and strangling him. But Cygnus, under divine protection, "had changed into the snowy bird whose name / He had while living." He flew away in the shape of a swan.

Not many were as lucky as he. The slaughter went on for more than nine years. The warriors, when they were not fighting, talked about fighting. They loved to listen to King Nestor, the oldest of the chieftains, and he had endless stories to tell them.

One of his favorites was the story of Caeneus, whose prowess was the more amazing because he was born a woman. As a lovely girl, he was raped by Neptune. The god "liked what he had taken," and asked her, "What do you want the most?" She answered that she never wanted to be so violated again; she wanted to stop being a woman. Neptune granted her wish.

Nestor claimed to have been alive for more than two hundred years—he probably meant two generations. He also claimed to have forgotten much, but his narrative belies that claim. He tells story upon story, and in endless detail. One of his longest tales concerns the Battle of the Centaurs.

Pirithous married Hippodame, and the centaurs (half-man, half-horse creatures), were invited to the wedding. One of them, Eurytus, lost his head and dragged the bride from the table. Soon everybody was fighting. Theseus tried to stop the outrage, but in vain. The horrible bloodshed went on until most centaurs were dead; only a few escaped. Even the young centaur lovers, Cyllarus and Hylonome, fell victim to the madness. Many Greeks fell, too, but Caeneus stood unharmed. Finally, the frenzied centaurs piled so many logs on him that he was crushed or suffocated.

After Nestor told this tale, Tlepolemus, the son of Hercules, challenged him to explain why he had omitted the deeds of Hercules in his account. The old king replied that he did so on purpose, because Hercules had killed his brothers. Nestor's silence was a form of revenge on Hercules.

While the Greek warriors slept after a night of storytelling, Neptune, ordinarily a champion of the Greeks, went to Apollo (main supporter of the Trojans) and suggested that the two of them take revenge on the Greeks for the death of Cygnus and other grievances. Apollo, glad to help the Trojans, instructed the cowardly

Paris to take aim at Achilles. The god directed the arrow to Achilles' one vulnerable spot, his heel, and so the Greeks' greatest hero was slain by the hand of a "coward and seducer." Truly, it would have been better if he had been killed by Penthesilea, the Amazon queen whom he had slain! After his corpse was burned, a fight arose among the Greek captains for his armor. The chief contenders were Ulysses and the Greater Ajax, son of Telamon. Agamemnon decided to call a council to arbitrate in the dangerous confrontation.

Analysis

The story of the Trojan War was, of course, the most famous event in Greek pre-history and it was, in fact, the beginning of their history as a nation. The story, with its innumerable details, was known by every schoolchild; the two great epics, the *Iliad* and the *Odyssey*, constituted their chief education. Ovid could take a great many things for granted, here only the briefest outline may be given.

At the wedding of Peleus and Thetis, all the gods were invited, except Eris, Discord, whom everyone disliked and feared. In revenge, she threw an apple into the gathering, inscribed "To the Fairest." Instantly, three goddesses claimed it for their own: Minerva, Juno, and Venus. The Trojan prince, Paris, was summoned to render judgment. The goddesses, though divinely beautiful, did not trust to their own charms and tried to bribe the judge. Paris, who wanted neither power nor wealth, succumbed to the bribe offered by Venus: to obtain the most beautiful woman in the world. This, as everyone knew, was Helen, Queen of Sparta, wife of Menelaus. Menelaus welcomed Paris when he came on a visit, and he trusted the ethic of hospitality to such a degree that he left him alone with his wife while he went away on a journey. When he discovered that in his absence Helen had eloped with his houseguest, he called upon the other chieftains, his allies bound to him by oath, to help him get his wife back.

Historians and mythographers alike have been speculating about the reasons for the eagerness with which the whole nation took up the cause. The oath was there, to be sure; but it has also been suggested that Troy, at its strategic location on the Hellespont, was an enticing prize to gain. King Priam was known to have untold riches. At any rate, the thousand ships were assembled under the leadership of Menelaus' brother, Agamemnon. When favorable winds failed, he was willing to sacrifice even his daughter Iphigenia. (His wife, unforgiving, killed him upon his return from the war.)

Just as Homer started the *Iliad*, boldly, *in medias res*, in the middle of things, Ovid moves quickly from the sacrifice of Iphigenia and a few opening skirmishes, to the rambling narrative of Nestor (touching upon a few highlights of the nine-year war based mainly on his personal recollections), to the anticlimactic death of Achilles. Ovid even risks poking gentle fun at old Nestor, who claims to have such a bad memory but remembers every confrontation, blow by blow. Nestor (and with him Ovid) seems more interested in the events at the wedding of Pirithous and Hippodame and the sex change of Cadneus than in the war itself.

Study Questions

1. Where did the Greek forces assemble before sailing for Troy?

2. What was the bad omen interpreted by Calchas?

3. What was the explanation of the invulnerability of Cygnus?

4. How does Nestor know all the details of the Battle of the Centaurs?

5. How did the other centaurs respond when Eurytus attacked the bride?

6. What happened to Phorbas, who lay, drunk and asleep, during the battle?

7. Why does Peleus appear so often in Nestor's tale?

8. What makes the death of Cyllarus and Hylonome so poignant?

9. Why did Neptune and Apollo conspire to make Paris the killer of Achilles?

10. What is meant by: "the same god armed and consumed" Achilles?

Answers

1. The Greek forces assembled at Aulis.

2. The bad omen was that a serpent ate a bird with its eight fledglings.

3. Cygnus was invulnerable because his father was the god Neptune.

4. Nestor was present at the wedding of Pirithous and Hippodame.

5. Once the bride was attacked, most of the other centaurs joined in the mêlée.

6. The sleeping Phorbas was also slain.

7. Nestor flatters Achilles with tales of his father's deeds.

8. The death of Cyllarus and Hylonome is a poignant "love death" of innocents.

9. Neptune and Apollo wanted to humiliate the Greeks.

10. Achilles' armor was made by the god Vulcan, smith of the gods; now he burns his dead body.

Suggested Essay Topics

1. There is a school of thought which maintains that, even though Homer wrote the greatest epic of the Greek nation, his real sympathies lay with the Trojans. Can you give examples of Ovid's "divided sympathies" also?

2. Comment on the relative magnitude of divine intervention in this Book compared to the earlier ones. How many miraculous transformations are there in Book Twelve?

Book XIII

New Characters:

Palamedes: *Greek warrior who tells tales about Ulysses and is cleverly betrayed by him*

Philoctetes: *friend of Hercules; heir to his bow and arrows*

Rhesus: *Thracian king; prevened from reaching Troy by Ulysses*

Dolon: *a Phrygian spy slain by Ulysses*

Helenus: *son of Priam with the gift of augury; captured by Ulysses*

Diomedes: *king of Argos; frequent companion of Ulysses*

Pyrrhus: *son of Achilles; his mother is a princess of Scyros, where Achilles was hidden to prevent him from going to war*

Teucer: *half-brother of Ajax; cousin of Achilles*

Telephus: *wounded then cured by Achilles*

Antenor: *Trojan chief, ready with Priam to return Helen to the Greeks*

Thersites: *a mean man; chastised by Ulysses*

Sarpedon: *son of Jove and Europa; cut down by Patroclus; harried by Ulysses*

Alastor, Chromius, Coeranos, Alcander, etc.: *victims of Ulysses*

Patroclus: *friend of Achilles who wears his armor; drives back Trojans but is slain by Hector*

Pleiades: *daughters of Atlas; a constellation represented on the shield of Achilles*

Orion: *a celebrated constellation*

Eurypylus, Thoas, Meriones: *Greek captains*

Cassandra: *Trojan princess whose prophecies are not believed*

Astyanax: *infant son of Hector; hurled from the battlements of Troy*

Trojan women: *abducted by the Greeks as the spoils of war*

Hecuba: *Queen of Troy; after the death of her last child, she turns into a dog and flees*

Polydorus: *a Trojan prince, sent by Priam to Thrace, and treacherously slain there*

Polymester: *a greedy ruler; murders Polydorus*

Polyxena: *youngest daughter of Hecuba; sacrificed to the hose of Achilles*

Aurora: *goddess of the dawn; mother of Memnon, a Trojan ally*

Aeneas: *son of the goddess venus by Anchises; a Trojan prince*

Ascanlus: *young son of Aeneas*

Anius: *priest of Apollo at Delphi*

Therses: *a guest of Anius*

Scylla: *now incarnated as a dangerous monster; later becomes a rock*

Charybdis: *a nymph; also a dangerous whirlpool opposite Scylla the rock*

Galatea: *a sea nymph, lover of Acis, pursued by the Cyclops Polyphemus*

Acis: *lover of Galatea; killed by Polyphemus; turned into a river*

Glaucus: *formerly a fisherman, now a river god; loves Scylla but is loved by Circe*

Circe: *an enchantress; falls in love with Glaucus, is rejected by him and punishes his beloved Scylla*

Oceanus and Tethys: *Titans who are ancestors of some of the gods*

Triton: *a sea god*

Summary

The Greek leaders and the people gathered to hear Ajax and Ulysses argue for the possession of the arms of Achilles. Ajax, deeply resentful for having to argue at all, and especially for having Ulysses as his adversary, starts by referring to his superior relatives, Jove being his grandfather, and Achilles his cousin. He ridicules Ulysses for having tried to evade service in the war, pretending madness. He criticizes Ulysses' role in the handling of Philoctetes, abandoning the wounded hero in Lemnos; the "planting" of false evidence on Palamedes, who had discovered his ruse of the pretended madness, and his desertion of Nestor. Ajax also recalls that he himself had once rescued Ulysses in his time of need and wishes he had not done so. Ajax points proudly to the fact that he had once knocked Hector himself down, and only the personal intervention of Jove had saved the Trojan champion. It was he, Ajax, who had saved the Greek ships in a time of rout. Then he enumerates Ulysses' accomplishments, products of lying, cheating, and stealing. He concludes with a challenge: throw the arms into the midst of the enemy ranks, and see who will bring them back.

The crowd only muttered until Ulysses rose to speak. He spoke eloquently and with graceful gestures. He seemed to brush away tears at the thought that the great Achilles himself was no longer able to wear his armor. But, Ulysses argued, the arms should go to the person who had brought Achilles to the war, meaning himself. As for his eloquence, he admits that he is a good speaker; not everyone can appear as stupid as Ajax.

Ulysses points to his own divine ancestors on both sides, but stresses that they don't count: worth alone does. If relationship would bestow claim to the arms, they should go to Achilles' son, Pyrrhus (by his other name Neoptolemus), or to his father Peleus, or his cousin Teucer. Instead, he enumerates his own accomplishments.

He reminds his listeners that Achilles' mother Thetis knew that if her son went to Troy, he would be killed there. She disguised him in a girl's dress and sent him to stay among women. But Ulysses, using a shield and spear as bait, drew the young man to himself and persuaded him to join the fight. Therefore, Ulysses argues, Achilles' heroic deeds should be added to those of his own, including the slaying of Hector.

Next, Ulysses reveals that it was he himself who had persuaded Agamemnon to sacrifice his daughter Iphigenia; and it was he who succeeded in bringing the girl to Aulis, by lying to her mother that Iphigenia would be married to Achilles. Furthermore, it was he, Ulysses, who went as ambassador to Troy and would have brought Helen back, had it not been for the refusal of the Trojan fanatics. He claims that it was he who had kept harassing the Trojans during the long siege and kept up the spirit of the discouraged Greek army. After the lying dream Jove sent to Agamemnon, and the consequent abandonment of the siege by the Greeks, says Ulysses, "it was I who stopped them; every victory since then should go to my credit."

He points to the friendship of the great Diomedes, the capture of the Trojan spy Solon, and the role he, Ulysses, had in defeating numerous Trojan allies. Throwing open his garment, Ulysses next displays his wounds—Ajax has none. As for the accomplishments

of Ajax, he distributes the glory by naming other heroes, in particular the dead Patroclus. Next he directly insults Ajax by claiming that Ajax is too ignorant to appreciate the beauty and significance of the arms of Achilles. As for his own initial reluctance to join the armies, he blames his loving wife, who, like the loving mother of Achilles, wished to protect a loved one.

Next, he defends his lying testimony against Palamedes—the Greeks now present had all consented to convict him. As for Philoctetes, Ulysses predicts that if anyone can persuade the wounded hero to join the war effort at this late time, it will be he, Ulysses. After all, it was he who captured Helenus, the Trojan soothsayer, thus obtaining valuable information; and it was he who stole the Palladium, the sacred effigy without which Troy could not have been taken (although he admits that Diomedes was his partner). He triumphantly announces, "a thinker always / Is better than a brave but stupid fighter....You are strong, and brainless; / I think about the future." If not to me, he said, give the arms to the true champion of our cause, Minerva!"

Ajax, out of humiliation, anger, and frustration, killed himself with his own sword. Out of his wounds, a crimson flower grew, like that which blossomed from Hyacinthus' blood.

Now, in possession of Achilles' arms, Ulysses sailed to obtain the bow and arrows of Hercules from Philoctetes. The wounded hero himself came along, and "the final blow / Was given, at last, to that long war. Troy fell, / And Priam fell....And Troy was burning." The bitter aftermath is given in broad strokes. Priam's wife lost her human shape; Cassandra was dragged by the hair; the women of Troy huddled fearfully, awaiting their brutal fate. Hector's precious child was hurled from the very tower from which he had watched his father's brave deeds. The Greek chiefs distributed the women among them as so many spoils.

After this brief overview, Ovid focuses on the tragedy of one person: Priam's aged queen, Hecuba. She alone had no taker (except the "crafty Ulysses" who thought it would be unwise to bring home a young woman. The other chiefs were not as wise). She hid in her bosom the ashes of her noble son Hector. Her only children not slain during and after the siege were Polydorus, sent across the strait to Thrace in order to safeguard some of the Trojan treasures, and Polyxena, her youngest daughter. She was hoping for the survival of at least those two. She did not know that Polydorus had been treacherously murdered by his host, Polymestor, and his body flung into the sea.

As the Greek fleet was gathering for departure, the angry ghost of Achilles appeared to them and demanded that the princess Polyxena be sacrificed to his memory. Accordingly, it was done. The royal maiden behaved with so much courage and dignity that even the priest who stabbed her to death shed tears. Hecuba, wishing to perform the last rites for her daughter, went to the seashore to fetch water, and there, to her horror, found the corpse of Polydorus.

Looking at his wounds, the mother steeled herself and asked for an audience with Polymestor, ostensibly to transmit some gold to her son. When the king continued to pretend that the gold would go to Polydorus, she attacked him, gouged out his eyes, and in her fury turned into a snarling dog. Even Juno admitted that Hecuba deserved no such misfortune.

Another grieving mother, Aurora, petitioned Jove for a fitting memorial for her slain son Memnon; the flames from his funeral pyre rose to heaven and eventually turned into birds, called "Memnon's daughters." Aurora herself, goddess of the Dawn, remembering her son, "dews the world with her tears."

"And yet the Fates did not permit Troy's hopes / To perish with her walls;" the son of Venus, Aeneas, was permitted to escape, carrying on his shoulders his aged father, Anchises, and leading his small son, Ascanius, by the hand. His ship took him to Delos where they enjoyed the hospitality of the priest Anius.

Anius told Aeneas the story of his daughters. Agamemnon had enslaved them. Two escaped, and eventually Bacchus metamorphosed them into doves. Next, Aeneas sought the counsel of the oracle of Apollo, who told him, "Seek your ancient mother!" After exchanging royal gifts Aeneas and his family moved on. Their adventurous journey at one time brought them to the point where Scylla and Charybdis endanger ships; Galatea, the nymph, was there also, and she told her story.

Galatea was in love with a handsome youth called Acis. But she was pursued by the Cyclops Polyphemus who sang ludicrous songs by way of wooing her. When she rejected him, he rose up threateningly. Galatea escaped by diving into the sea, but Acis was turned into a river. Scylla, meanwhile, had her own unfortunate tale. She was accosted by Glaucus, the fisherman who, by chewing on an herb, had been transformed into a sea-god. Scylla fled him, and he, in anger, went to the halls of Circe, daughter of the Sun.

Analysis

Book Thirteen is probably the most brilliant of all the books of the *Metamorphoses*. Its first part condenses most of the famous episodes of the *Iliad* (with some notable exceptions), told from the point of view of the two contenders for the arms of Achilles, the Greater Ajax and Ulysses. It continues with the heartbreaking account of the Fall of Troy and its aftermath, including the fates of the survivors. Then, in the last part, the tone changes from that of majestic tragedy to one of travel adventures, lighthearted romance, and even farce. The total effect is unlike that of any other Book in this long poem, but the principle was known to the ancient Greeks who interspersed farcical "satyr-plays" to relieve the pitiful and terrible effects of their tragedies.

The great debate between Ajax and Ulysses is in the epic tradition, but Ovid dazzles with his version, which makes use of just about every device known to the practitioners of rhetoric; he also demonstrates the fact that sincere anger, as displayed by Ajax, is no match for clever manipulation of the audience, as demonstrated by his opponent. Ulysses knows how to play on the emotions of his audience and to influence the votes of those who count. Ovid, in reporting the scene, short-circuits the aftermath; he omits the sordid details of the madness of Ajax mentioned by other ancient authors.

Because the story of the Fall of Troy was so well known, from the Homeric poems and from Virgil as well as from Greek tragedy and lyric poetry, Ovid limits himself to just a few incidents, but he achieves maximum rhetorical and pathetic effect. The transformation of Hecuba into a dog, and the reference to her tomb as "The Bitch's Tomb" or "Dogsbarrow," is in the ancient tradition and probably reflects a pre-Hellenic mythic survival; Robert Graves equates the unfortunate queen with Hecate, Goddess of Death; her metamorphosis also invokes analogies with the Egyptian god of the dead, Anubis, similarly represented with the head of a dog.

The mourning of Memnon by his mother Aurora, according to Professor Kenney, can be seen as a complement to the Cygnus episode, rounding out the Trojan section with a bird-metamorphosis, the way it started, making it symmetrical, as it were. This shows the conscious artistry of Ovid as "architect" of his poem.

The argument certainly seems to have merit, for at this point Ovid makes his second big shift in subject-matter, his second break in the plot of the poem. Now begins Part III: The Story of Rome and Its Antecedents.

Ovid picks up the theme already venerably established by Virgil and shows how, after the Fall of Troy, the goddess Venus, mother of Aeneas, rescued him and enabled him to escape the burning ruins. By carrying his aged father and leading his young son, Aeneas is shown to be securely established in the continuity of the generations. There was an oral tradition, utilized by Virgil, that Dardanus, ancestor of the Trojans, came from Latium, in present-day Italy. Therefore, Aeneas, one of only two surviving Trojan princes (the other was Helenus, a minor character), had to be led back to his "mother."

Having started him on his journey, Ovid now lightens the tone by the description of the festivities on the island of Delos and two pursuit-accounts: that of Galatea by Polyphemus and Scylla by Glaucus. The wooing of Galatea, a favorite subject of Renaissance painters, contains Ovid's funniest passage, the Song of Polyphemus, moving the poem "from the sublime to the ridiculous," as it were, and thus providing emotional release after so much tragic tension.

Study Questions

1. In what mood did Ajax begin his argument about the armor?

2. From start to finish, what was his attitude toward Ulysses?

3. What arguments were used by both competitors to promote their claims?

4. How does Ulysses justify his not-always-honest methods?

5. How does Ovid characterize the outcome of the debate?

6. Quote the paradox summing up Ajax' fate.

7. What provided the final blow to Troy?

8. What fate did Hecuba fear most?

9. What outrage did Agamemnon commit against a noncombatant, the priest Anius?

10. By what means does Ovid characterize the uncouthness of Polyphemus?

Answers

1. Ajax is angry and belligerent, resentful that he has to prove anything.

2. He despises Ulysses, calling him a liar and a thief.

3. Both competitors cited their divine ancestors and their heroic deeds.

4. Ulysses points out that his methods worked; they were also supported by the other chiefs.

5. "The eloquent man bore off / The brave man's arms."

6. "Unconquered, he was conquered by his sorrow."

7. The bow and arrows of Hercules, inherited by Philoctetes, arrived.

8. Only Ulysses claimed her, an old woman, as his prize. She was afraid of the humiliation of becoming a servant of Penelope, the wife of Ulysses.

9. Agamemnon dragged off the daughters of Anius to feed his armies.

10. The Song of Polyphemus is at once pathetic and humorous both in content and diction.

Suggested Essay Topics

1. Ulysses, as depicted by Ovid, is very different from the Ulysses depicted by Homer in the *Iliad* and the *Odyssey*. In those two poems, while "resourceful," he is basically worthy of admiration and respect. The reader's sympathy tends to be generally with him, even when he is cruel (as with Polyphemus) or savage (as with the suitors of his wife). After all, he is fighting for his life and kingdom. In this Book, both in the portrayal by Ajax and by the account given of his actions by Ovid himself, he is a far-from-sympathetic character. Give instances.

2. Euripides, the great Greek playwright, wrote a tragedy, *The Trojan Women*. From your reading of this Book, which scenes would you think constituted the plot of that tragedy, Euripides' anti-war manifesto?

Book XIV

New Characters:

Dido: *queen of Carthage*

Acestes: *a Sicilian king of Trojan descent*

Iris: *messenger of Juno*

Sibyl (Sibylla): *priestess of Apollo at his temple*

Caieta: *old nurse of Aeneas*

Macareus: *companion of Ulysses*

Achaemenides: *companion of Ulysses*

Aeolus: *king of the winds*

Antiphates: *king of the Lestrygonians*

Polites, Eurylochus and Elpenor: *messengers of Ulysses to Circe*

Cyllenius: *Mercury; named after his birthplace*

Picus: *son of Saturn, a local god*

Canens: *a nymph loved by Picus*

Turnus: *a king of the Rutuli in Italy, and a rival of Aeneas for Lavinia's hand*

Evander (Euander): *an ally of Aeneas*

Venulus: *a messenger sent by Turnus to Diomedes*

Acmon: *companion of Diomedes; changed into a bird by Venus*

Iulus: *another name for Ascanius, the son of Aeneas*

Indiges: *the name under which the deified Aeneas was worshipped*

Silvius, Latinus, Alba, Epytus, Capys, Capetus, Tiberinus: *rulers after Iulus*

Acrota: *son of Tibernus*

Romulus: *son of Mars; founder of Rome*

Aventinus and Procas: *famous rulers*

Pomona and Vertumnus: *native deities of growth and fertility*

Iphis: *a young man of common origins who is in love with the princess Anaxarete*

Numitos: *a Roman king*

Ausonia: *Italy*

Amulius: *son of Numitor; deposes his father; is deposed by Romulus*

Pales: *goddess of herds*

Tatius: *Sabine king who warred with Romulus but later shares power with him*

Tarpeia: *Roman maid who opened the gates to the Sabines and is killed by the,*

Cures: *a Sabine city*

Ilia (Rhea Sylvia): *daughter of Numitor; mother of Romulus with Mars*

Quirinus: *the name Romulus carries after his apotheosis*

Hersilia: *widow of Pomulus; known as Hora after her apotheosis*

Summary

Glaucus, the fisherman turned sea-god, rejected by Schylla, asked for the help of Circe, the daughter of the Sun and an accomplished sorceress. Instead of helping him to win Scylla, Circe offered herself to him. He declined; Circe vented her anger on the nymph, changing her into a horrid monster. Scylla had harried Ulysses' crew, snatching some of his seamen, but by the time the Trojan ships arrived, she had turned into a rock, dreaded by sailors.

Avoiding Scylla and Charybdis, Aeneas and his fleet had almost reached western Italy when the winds blew them to the Lybian coast. The Sidonian queen, Dido, received them cordially, fell in love with Aeneas, and, when he had to leave her, immolated herself. Aeneas went back to Sicily, honored his father's grave, and after some adventures arrived at the cave of the Sibyl of Cumae. With her help, he descended to the nether world and saw the shade of his father. She also told him her story. As a beautiful virgin, she was wooed by Apollo, who offered to fulfill any wish of hers. She asked for a long life—but failed to specify that she should live them as a young woman. Now she was seven hundred years old and had to endure three hundred more miserable years.

Achaemenides, a Greek whom Aeneas had saved and who was now traveling with them, later met an old comrade by the name of Macareus, another former fellow sailor of Ulysses. They exchanged stories of their adventures. Achaemenides related that he was left behind at the time that Ulysses succeeded in eluding Polyphemus after blinding him. Much later, he had been seen and rescued by Aeneas, a Trojan saving a Greek! Macareus was another survivor: he managed to escape when the Lestrygonians hurled rocks on the fleet of Ulysses, went with him to Circe's island, was turned into a pig together with his comrades, but was saved by Ulysses and his magic herb, moly, the gift of Mercury. Ulysses became the lover of Circe, and they all stayed there for a year.

While on Circe's island, Macareus continued, he had heard some interesting tales. He related one of them: the story of Picus. Picus was the son of Saturn, the ancient Titan, grandfather of Jove. Picus was handsome and much pursued by nymphs and naiads, but his heart belonged to one only, a nymph by the name of Canens. Circe wanted to seduce him, but he was steadfast; in her anger, she turned him into a woodpecker. Canens searched for him far and wide and eventually literally dissolved in tears. Macareus added that Circe had told them so many fearful tales of the dangers of the homeward journey that he decided not to accompany Ulysses but to stay there, on the western coast of Italy, where they met him. Aeneas buried his old nurse, Caieta, and the place is still named after her, Gaeta.

Heeding the warning of Macareus, Aeneas avoided Circe's island, made for the mouth of the river Tiber, where he won a bride and a kingdom. He had to fight with a rival for the hand of his wife and for his new country. It was fortunate that his rival, Turnus, received no help from Diomedes, to whom he applied. In giving his excuses, Diomedes told his story to the messenger of Turnus.

Diomedes recounted the adventures he had after the Fall of Troy. Since the Lesser Ajax had ravished a virgin priestess,

Cassandra, Minerva withdrew her favor from the Greeks; they were all in danger of drowning. Venus was especially angry with Diomedes, who had wounded her in battle as she was trying to save Aeneas, her son. Acmon, one of Diomedes' men, insulted Venus further, she turned him and his cohorts into birds. So now, Diomedes explained, he was unable to come to the aid of Turnus.

The unsuccessful messenger, Venulus, on his return trip, made fun of some nymphs and was turned into a wild olive-tree, his tongue's bitterness immortalized in the bitter taste of the fruit.

Next Turnus tried to torch the Trojan ships, but the holy mother, Cybele, prevented this; instead, she metamorphosed the ships into playful naiads. These water sprites hated Greeks; they were happy when Ulysses suffered a shipwreck, and also later, when the vessel that had taken him home to Ithaca turned to stone.

The war went on, the adversaries fighting, "Not for a kingdom, dowry, a bride, or scepter, / They fought, but victory only, and the shame / Of losing kept them fighting." However, at last Venus saw victory come to her son. The formerly mighty town of Turnus, Ardea, was destroyed by fire, and from its ashes a black heron flew up.

Such was the power of the goodness of Aeneas, that even vindictive Juno gave up her hatred of him. His son, Iulus, was now grown, ready to take over the country. Venus arranged for the deification of her son, and now he is a god under the name of Indiges, the Native-Born. He was followed by a series of kings; gardens and fruitful fields were established. The god of fertility, Vertumnus, fell in love with the goddess of gardens, Pomona, and, wooing her in the disguise of a woman, told her the story of Iphis and Anaxarete.

Iphis, a youth of common birth, dared to love a princess, Anaxarete, who spurned him. At last, he hanged himself at her door, but when she saw his dead body, she looked on so coldly that she turned into a marble statue.

Pomona was not impressed with the tale, or the disguise, but when she saw Vertumnus in his own radiant beauty, she returned his love.

The state, now still called Ausonia, survived the treason of Amulius, who dethroned his father Numitor. Numitor was helped by his grandson, Romulus, and the City walls were built. Tatius, king of the Sabines, was the next to attack; a local maid, Tarpeia, helped the enemy in expectation of a reward but instead was killed by the Sabine warriors. Venus helped the people of Romulus; there was terrible bloodshed, but eventually peace was established. After his death, Romulus was deified under the name of Quirinus. His widow, Hersilia, mourned him so much that Juno sent Iris down with words of consolation and an invitation to follow. The noble queen, too, became a divinity under the name of Hora.

Analysis

After the magnificence of Book Thirteen, Book Fourteen presents an anticlimax. Ovid crowds too much material into it, and he is hampered by the fact that much of the story of Aeneas and his heirs was already told by Virgil, and told supremely well. Like his hero, Aeneas, he has to avoid a double danger: the Scylla of saying too much and the Charybdis of not saying enough. The perfunctory way with which he moves Aeneas from Delos to Carthage, to Sicily, and along the coast of Western Italy is almost painful to read; even the most careful reader is hard put to establish, for instance, where the two former comrades of Ulysses met, or what the point of their exchange is, apart from padding the tale with materials borrowed from the *Odyssey*.

It is not only geography that bores Ovid: Roman pre-history does also. The Romans counted the years *ab urbe condita,* from the Founding of the City. The early rulers of the country, which prior to Romulus had as yet no real name, were themselves no more than names—all fictitious, of course. Ovid's imagination, so fertile when dealing with nymphs and naiads, deserted him when dealing with these ciphers from the past, whom he did not feel brave enough to ignore, but about whom he found it difficult to say anything new. The censors of Caesar Augustus were too close at hand, so, he had to content himself with platitudes.

To make matters worse, the extra incidents with which he tries to enrich the Virgilian plot-line fit poorly. The story of Pomona and Vertumnus is inserted too abruptly; the tales of Picus and Canens and of Iphis and Anaxarete are weaker versions of earlier, better stories of transformations. Ovid seems to have been in a hurry to reach his required conclusion: the glorious establishment of the Roman Empire.

Study Questions

1. According to the myth, Circe was the aunt of Medea. What similarities do you find in their characters ?

2. Explain the allusion that Venus, "angry about her father's gossiping, / Had made her (Circe) what she was."

3. The story of Aeneas and Dido, one of the chief plot elements of the *Aeneid* of Virgil, is told by Ovid in half a dozen lines. What effect, if any, do they have on the reader?

4. What well-known theme is repeated in the story of the wish of the Sibyl?

5. What great change has occurred in the fate of the Cyclops, Polyphemus, since his last appearance in the poem?

6. What common motifs appear in the tales about Scylla and about Canens?

7. How does Ovid manage to explain the appearance of a Greek chieftain, Diomedes, on Italian soil?

8. Why is Diomedes unable to help Turnus?

9. Why did the great goddess, Cybele, prevent Turnus from burning the ships of Aeneas?

10. How does the ending of the tale of Vertumnus and Pomona differ from that of the usual tales about lustful divinities?

Answers

1. Medea and Circe were both sorceresses. Their methods were similar; so was their motivation. Both acted out of fury when rejected by the men of their choice. Both punished their "rivals" by poison.

2. Circe was the daughter of the Sun-god, and Venus was once betrayed by his tattling on her.

3. The love-death of Dido and Aeneas' betrayal of her were among the most celebrated scenes of ancient literature. Ovid's version makes little or no impression on the reader.

4. The Sibyl's story is another in the series of the Foolish Wish.

5. Since the time of his wooing of Galatea, Polyphemus had his eye poked out by Ulysses.

6. Both Canens and Scylla were victims of Circe's spiteful revenge for being scorned by men she wanted for herself.

7. Diomedes explains that he married a local heiress.

8. Having been punished by Venus, Diomedes lost most of his men.

9. Cybele did not wish to have her precious trees burned. An early example of conservation effort, similar to the one in *The Epic of Gilgamesh*, in which Gilgamesh is punished for cutting down the Cedars of Lebanon. He loses his claim to immortality.

10. While Vertumnus if fully prepared to rape Pomona, the situation is saved when she, in her turn, is attracted to him.

Suggested Essay Topics

1. Discuss the effect of the rather sudden change of scene from Greece and Troy to Italy and the Western Mediterranean.

2. Because Ovid assumes the reader's familiarity with Aeneas and his descendants, his characterizations of them are largely perfunctory. In view of this, how do you feel about the three deifications described in this Book?

Book XV

New Characters:

Numa: *king of Rome after Quirinis*

Croton: *hero who entertained Hercules; namesake of Crotona*

Myscelus: *founder of Crotona*

Pythagoras: *Greek philosopher; born in Samos and migrated to Crotona*

Euphorbus: *a brave Trojan who is killed*

Helenus: *advises Aeneas about the future*

Thyestes: *brother of Atreus—fed on the flesh of his sons*

Egeria: *wife of Numa*

Hippolytus: *son of Theseus and the Ammazon Hippolyta; tells his story to Egeria*

Phaedra: *stepmother of Theseus*

Paeon: *son of Apollo; inherits the god's healing power and applies it to Aesculapius*

Virbius: *the name by whick Hippolytus is known after his rebirth*

Tages: *a deity sprung from a clod*

Cipus: *a Roman who refused the kingship*

Aesculapius (Asclepius; Imhotep): *son of Apollo, god of healing*

Caesar: *family name of Julius Caesar; presumably descended from Iulus, the son of Aeneas*

Caesar Augustus: *adopted son and heir of Julius Caesar*

Vesta: *goddess of hearth and home*

Summary

After the death and deification of Romulus, a successor had to be chosen. It was the famous Numa. He traveled to Crotona, in southern Italy, to acquire the wisdom taught there by Pythagoras. Inquiring about the history of Crotona, he was informed that Hercules had once been hospitably received there by the hero Croton; Hercules promised him that ages hence a city would be founded there. The actual founder was an Argive hero called Myscelus, who was urged in a dream to leave his city and fulfill his destiny. In spite of a prohibition against emigration, Myscelus made his plans to obey the divine command and would have been put to death except for a miracle by Hercules. He undertook the journey and built the city. This was the beginning of *Magna Graecia*, extensive Greek settlements in what is now Italy.

Pythagoras was an exile who made his home in Crotona. He was born on the island of Samos but fled from the dictatorship then in power there. He was a great philosopher and teacher. People

listened to him eagerly, especially when he explained to them the origins of things. He was also the first person to teach that animal foods should not be eaten. He advocated a return to the Golden Age, when men ate only the fruits of the Earth. It had been a good-for-nothing, Pythagoras declared, who incited humans to imitate lions and other carnivores; this paved the way to crime. Once the killing of dangerous beasts was condoned, excuses were found to slaughter pigs and goats also, claiming that they damaged plant life. But what excuse can be found for killing the innocent sheep, which harm no one but provide us with wool and milk? Surely they are worth more alive than dead! Or what can justify the slaughter of oxen, man's faithful comrades in tilling the soil? How bewildered the ox stands there, just before he is killed as a sacrifice! The very barley he helped to grow is sprinkled at him, and, uncompre-hending, he sees the priest's knife flashing as he is slain. His entrails are examined for omens, and then men feast upon his flesh. "Do not do this, / I pray you, but remember: when you taste / The flesh of slaughtered cattle, you are eating / Your fellow-workers."

The teachings of Pythagoras also led men to the mysteries of Apollo. No one else had ever revealed them before. There is no reason to fear death: "Our souls / Are deathless; always, when they leave our bodies, / They find new dwelling-places." Pythagoras well remembered his last previous life: he was known as Euphorbus, fought at Troy, and was killed by Menelaus. Just recently, in Juno's temple in Argos, he recognized the shield he had carried in that incarnation. "All things are always changing, / But nothing dies." Since the spirit comes and goes, shifts residence but always keeps on living—like the pliant wax that changes form but always remains wax—we must not murder animals, lest we become guilty of fratricide.

The revelations received from Apollo, continued Pythagoras, enable him to fly freely through the air. "Full sail, I voyage / Over the boundless ocean, and I tell you / Nothing is permanent in all the world; / All things are fluent; every image forms, / Wandering through change. Time is itself a river / In constant movement...." Day turns to night, the seasons revolve endlessly, and our bodies change, from youth to old age. Even the elements change, "but the great sum is constant."

Pythagoras lists "example on example" of changes: mountain tops which were once underwater, cities which are now covered by sea, rivers which have changed their courses and have amazing qualities, and many more. He does not believe every story he hears, of course, but there are certainly some very strange things which are well attested. Cocoons turn into moths, frogs jump out of the mud, and bear-cubs, originally just little lumps, are licked into shape by the mother. And how many different birds can hatch from eggs—peacocks, eagles, doves! Wonders! The phoenix can renew itself; the hyena is bisexual, coral is pliant under water but hard upon exposure to air.

World history is also a witness to change. Consider Troy, that great and wonderful city, now a heap of ruins! Pythagoras, the former Euphorbus, remembers from his former incarnation how Helenus, the augur, had consoled Aeneas, predicting that Troy will not wholly perish. One of the descendants of Aeneas will make his new city "empress / Of the whole world, and after earth has used him / The heavens will enjoy him, Heaven will be / His destination." Pythagoras expressed his satisfaction to Numa that the prophecy of Helenus was coming true, "That the Greek victory was to such good purpose."

Pythagoras summed up his main teachings: we are all changing. But death is not the end. "We are not bodies only, / But winged spirits, with the power to enter / Animal forms, house in the bodies of cattle." Therefore, we must respect animals as members of our own families, and never eat meat. The habit of eating animal food is wicked in itself; it is also cruel to innocent creatures.

Numa returned to Latium and reigned peacefully. After a long reign, he died. His wife Egeria mourned for him so bitterly that she fled the city, hiding in Aricia, at a shrine sacred to Diana. Her weeping disturbed the goddess, and Egeria was visited by Hippolytus, who tried to console her by relating the story of his own reincarnation.

Hippolytus, son of Theseus by the Amazon Queen Hippolyta, was hated by his stepmother Phaedra, whose advances he rejected. She pretended that it was he who had tried to seduce her. Theseus believed her; in his anger he asked the god Neptune to punish his son. Neptune obliged; he sent a giant wave which upset the chariot of Hippolytus, and the young man drowned. But Paeon, son of Apollo, god of healing, restored him to life. Diana transformed him, placed him in her sacred grove, and changed his name to Virbius.

Egeria was not comforted, and Diana metamorphosed her into a fountain. This change was as startling as the appearance of Tages, an Etrurian deity, in a field being ploughed, or as the spear of Romulus which took root and became a tree. Cipus, too, was amazed when he saw horns growing on his forehead. The people wanted to make him king, but he refused.

Ovid now invokes the Muses to help him tell the arrival of Aesculapius in Rome. After a plague, the Romans asked Apollo's help, who directed them to his son, then being worshipped at Epidaurus, in Greece. The god appeared to the delegation in a dream and promised to help them. He did accompany them in the form of a giant serpent and finally, arriving in Rome, "put on his heavenly form again," and brought health to Latium.

In contrast with Aesculapius, who came to Rome from foreign lands, Caesar "Is a god in his own city. First in war, / And first in peace"; he is the newest star in Heaven, but above all he is immortal through his son. All his victories pale beside the fact that he is the father of the present emperor. He had to become a god. Venus saw the mortal danger he was in, being plotted against, and appealed to Heaven to save him, but Jove explained to her that the Fates cannot be moved. "He has finished / The time allotted him....But he will enter / the Heaven as god." Under his son, the world will at last have peace. There are several precedents for sons being greater than the fathers; this is such a case. May the new Caesar rule long!

In the Epilogue, Ovid declares, "Now I have done my work. It will endure, / I trust..../ Beyond Time's hunger...part of me, / The better part, immortal, will be borne / Above the stars; my name will be remembered. / I shall be read, and through all centuries, / I shall be living, always."

Analysis

This, the last book of the *Metamorphoses*, has two main parts. One, the teachings of Pythagoras, was perhaps the part of the entire poem that was closest to Ovid's own heart. He poured his most passionate thought into it, infused it with his most affecting imagery, and clothed it with his most fluent poetry. The other main part of Book Fifteen contains an account of the development of Roman history, the deification of Caesar, and a hymn of praise to Augustus. In that part, his tone is harder to define; some critics feel he is being sarcastic; perhaps he is just being diplomatic.

After a brief account of the founding of Crotona, Ovid introduces the great figure of Pythagoras. Apart from Caesar and Augustus, both of whom are treated as more divine than human, Pythagoras is the only fully historical character in the poem. An exile from the tyranny of Samos, he settled in present-day Italy and taught there. Not only was he a famous philosopher, teacher, and mathematician (author of the Pythagorean theorem, among his contributions), he also founded a school and had a cult following which survived him. His disciples, women as well as men, followed his lifestyle of strict vegetarianism and non-violence. In his book, *The Greeks and the Irrational*, Professor E. R. Doods attributes to him the introduction into Greek thought of the very concept of the soul. Prior to Pythagoras, the Greeks knew only of a kind of animal soul, and the vague entity known as a ghost or shade; but a soul which survives independently of the body, is able to soar freely, learn divine mysteries, and penetrate into all regions of heaven and the underworld was an idea which Pythagoras learned from the shamans north of the Black Sea (Hyperborean Apollo). Pythagoras implanted this higher soul-concept into the Greek consciousness in the specific form of *metempsychosis*, the transmigration of the soul.

Ovid presents Pythagoras as the teacher of the second king of Rome, Numa. This is a historical impossibility, since Numa lived about two hundred years (eighth century B.C.) before Pythagoras (sixth century B.C.). Ovid employed poetic license in connecting his ideal philosopher with his ideal ruler. In his presentation of the teachings of Pythagoras, Ovid also included all other philosophical tenets that appealed to him, such as those found in Epicurus, Lucretius, and Heraclitus. In the great monologue attributed to Pythagoras, he finally stated the underlying theme of the whole *Metamorphoses*: all is in constant flux, all things always change.

The story of Hippolytus is designed to illustrate the truth of the doctrine of metempsychosis: it was a favorite of ancient storytellers and the subject of several classical works. The myths concerning Theseus and his family were the inspiration for plays by Euripides and Seneca (*Hippolytus*), the French playwright Racine (*Phèdre*), as well as the setting of Shakespeare's *A Midsummer Night's Dream*, which is supposed to take place on the occasion of "the marriage of Theseus and Hippolyta." The cult of Virbius at Aricia, not far from Rome, survived into modern times, as documented in Sir James Frazer's seminal book on mythology, *The Golden Bough.*

The tale of Cipus is more difficult to justify at this point except as an allusion that Julius Caesar, too, refused the kingship. It makes one wonder whether Ovid is writing this tongue-in-cheek; it is true that Caesar had refused the kingship, but he had allowed himself to be made into an Emperor; in fact, his family name came to mean "emperor."

Aesculapius is introduced as a counterweight to Caesar: as the healing god saved Rome from the plague, so Julius saved Rome from civil war. The fact that Ovid now emphatically calls upon the Muses shows the importance of the coming episodes: the apotheosis of Julius Caesar and the glories of the present regime. To what extend Ovid felt the noose tightening about his neck (his coming exile) is hard to establish; the servile tone he assumes toward Augustus is highly uncharacteristic.

Only in the Epilogue does he reassert his dignity as he confidently announces his future immortality. The "better part of him," his soul, will survive, as Pythagoras, the great exile had taught. But he goes beyond this. His name will survive all through the ages: his poem will be read. In this confident stance he is in good company: Horace, Shakespeare, and Archibald MacLeish have expressed the same idea about their own literary work. And there is great truth in it: the *Metamorphoses* is read; Ovid lives.

Study Questions

1. What was the role of Hercules in the history of Crotona?

2. What was the significance of the founding of Crotona?

3. What were the two main teachings of Pythagoras?

4. What personal testimony did Pythagoras give of metempsychosis?

5. To what episode in the *Metamorphoses* does "Salmacis" allude to?

6. Identify the allusions to Delos, the Argo, and the Clashing Rocks.

7. How could Pythagoras "remember" what Helenus told Aeneas?

8. What is the intention of Hippolytus in talking to Egeria?

9. Where is Etruria?

10. Why was Venus so interested in the destiny of Caesar?

Answers

1. Hercules predicted that a city would be founded on that spot.

2. Crotona was the first Greek settlement in Italy proper.

3. Pythagoras taught vegetarianism and metempsychosis.

4. Pythagoras claimed to remember his previous life as a Trojan.

5. Ovid relates the story of the pool Salmacis in Book Four.

6. The myth of the Argonauts is told in Books Five and Six.

7. Euphorbus was dead by the time of Helenus' prophecy; the only way he could "remember" it was through divine revelation by Apollo.

8. Hippolytus tries to console Egeria by suggesting that Numa still lives, though in a different incarnation.

9. Etruria is the present-day Tuscany, in Italy.

10. Julius Caesar traced his descent from Iulus, Aeneas' son.

Suggested Essay Topics

1. Summarize the teachings of Pythagoras concerning the killing and eating of animals.

2. Summarize the teachings of Pythagoras concerning change in general and metempsychosis in particular.

Sample Analytical Paper Topics

The following paper topics are designed to test your understanding of the play as a whole and analyze important themes and literary devices. Following each question is a sample outline to help you get started.

Topic #1

On one level, the *Metamorphoses* may be taken as a *literal* explanation of the origin of things; compare and contrast the Graeco-Roman creation myths with the Judeo-Christian Genesis accounts.

Outline

I. Thesis Statement: *The Graeco-Roman and Judeo-Christian accounts of creation have numerous points suitable for comparison and contrast.*

II. The Graeco-Roman creation myths as related by Ovid

    A. The creation out of Chaos

    B. The differentiation of things

        1. Heaven from earth

        2. Water from land

        3. Air from stratosphere

        4. Further subdivision

III.   The Judeo-Christian traditions of creation as told in the Bible

    A.   The Creation in Genesis 1:1–2:4

    B.   The Creation in Genesis 2:4–2:25

IV.   There are numerous similarities between the two traditions

    A.   Both show that the original chaos was changed by a creator

    B.   Both show that the creation occurred in stages

V.   The two traditions also show many differences

    A.   In Graeco-Roman: the identity of the creator is uncertain

    B.   Judeo-Christian: God created everything

Topic #2

The Greek and Roman gods show many moral failings and lack of sympathy toward humans. Show examples of their behavior which appear reprehensible to us.

Outline

I.   Thesis Statement: *Despite the Graeco-Roman divinities numerous moral failings, such as sexual rapaciouness, adultery, and jealousy, the gods still kept their promises.*

II.   The moral failings of the Graeco-Roman divinities

    A.   Sexual rapaciousness of male divinities

        1.   Rape of numerous virgins by Jove, Apollo, Neptune, Pan, etc.

        2.   Indifference toward their victims by Mercury, Achelous, etc.

        3.   Deceit, lies, disguises in obtaining their objectives

    B.   Sexual rapaciousness of female divinities

        1.   Aurora's pursuit of Cephalus

        2.   Echo's pursuit of Narcissus

     3.   Salmacis' pursuit of Hermaphroditus

     4.   Circe's seduction of Ulysses and pursuit of Glaucus and Picus

  C. Adultery by divinities condoned by other gods: Mars and Venus

  D. Jealousy of rivals, vengeance on their families and whole cities

     1.   Juno's cruelty to Jove's sexual victims

     2.   Juno's cruelty to family members and clans of Jove's victims

     3.   Juno's cruelty to others who displease her

     4.   Minerva's jealousy and vengeance toward those who displease her

     5.   Minerva's treachery, pretending to be Hector's brother

     6.   Violence and rage of Neptune, with or without reason

     7.   Caprice of the gods, especially the Fates

III. The one rule which binds the gods is that they must keep their promises—even if by doing so they destroy the petitioner

  A. Phaethon

  B. Semele

  C. Sibyl

  D. Midas

Topic #3

The *reasons* for the metamorphoses are inconsistent. Some were inflicted on people or lesser divinities (nymphs, etc.) as punishments for some transgression, others out of spite; some were performed in order to rescue someone from danger. Some transformations occurred because they seemed appropriate to the person transformed; some seemed to have no good reason at all, and some metamorphoses were *apotheoses*, conferring divine status on a mortal. In addition, Ovid mentions *changes* in nature, requiring no special divine intervention. Give examples of each.

Outline

I.   Thesis Statement: *Transformations occur in many forms in* Metamorphoses. *Some are the results of punishments for transgressions. Other are the result of vengeful and spiteful behavior, and others are unmotivated and unexplained. However, despite there differences, they all prove the maxim: "Everything always changes."*

II.   Punishments for transgressions

    A.   Sins or crimes committed out of wickedness

    B.   Transgressions committed in innocence or by accident

III.   Gods acting out of spite, personal vendetta, jealousy, etc.

    A.   Divinities acting out of spite or pique

    B.   Divinities carrying out a vendetta against persons or clans

    C.   Gods or goddesses acting against competitors

IV.   Metamophoses which were occasioned by unusual behavior, e.g., diving

V.   Capricious, unmotivated, or unexplained reasons for changes

VI.   Apotheoses of heroes as rewards for exceptional merit

VII.   Metamorphoses requiring no special divine intervention; natural changes

SECTION FOUR

Bibliography

Quotations from *Metamorphoses* are taken from the following translation:

Ovid *Metamorphoses*. Translated by Rolfe Humphries. Bloomington: Indiana University Press, 1955.

Other Sources:

Anderson, William S. *Ovid's Metamorphoses*. Books 6–10. Norman: University of Oklahoma Press, 1972.

Dodds, E. R. *The Greeks and the Irrational*. Boston: Beacon Press, 1957.

Graves, Robert. *The Greek Myths*. I–II. Baltimore: Penguin Books, 1955.

Graves, Robert. *The White Goddess*. New York: Random House, 1948.

Hamilton, Edith. *Mythology*. Boston: Little, Brown, 1942.

Hill, D. E. *Ovid: Metamorphoses* I–IV. Oak Park: Bolchazy-Carducci, 1985.

Kenney, Edwin J., ed. and notes; tr. A. D. Melville. *Ovid: Metamorphoses*. Oxford: 1986.

Kerenyi, C. *The Gods of the Greeks*. Vanguard: Evergreen.

Miller, Frank Justus. *Ovid in Six Volumes*. IV: *Metamorphoses*. Cambridge: Harvard University Press, 136, 1976.